TALES OF
NORSE
MYTHOLOGY

 "Cease, strange Vanir........
cease your rough play"

TALES OF
NORSE
MYTHOLOGY

A. & E. KEARY
ILLUSTRATED BY C. E. BROCK

FALL RIVER PRESS

New York

FALL RIVER PRESS

New York

An Imprint of Sterling Publishing
387 Park Avenue South
New York, NY 10016

This 2013 facsimile edition published by Fall River Press.
Originally published as *The Heroes of Asgard* in 1857.

ISBN 978-1-4351-4385-2 (print format)
ISBN 978-1-4351-4438-5 (ebook)

Distributed in Canada by Sterling Publishing
C/o Canadian Manda Group, 165 Dufferin Street
Toronto, Ontario, Canada M6K 3H6
Distributed in the United Kingdom by GMC Distribution Services
Castle Place, 166 High Street, Lewes, East Sussex, England BN7 1XU
Distributed in Australia by Capricorn Link (Australia) Pty. Ltd.
P.O. Box 704, Windsor, NSW 2756, Australia

For information about custom editions, special sales, and premium and
corporate purchases, please contact Sterling Special Sales at 800-805-5489
or specialsales@sterlingpublishing.com.

Manufactured in the United States of America

2 4 6 8 10 9 7 5 3 1

www.sterlingpublishing.com

CONTENTS

ILLUSTRATIONS

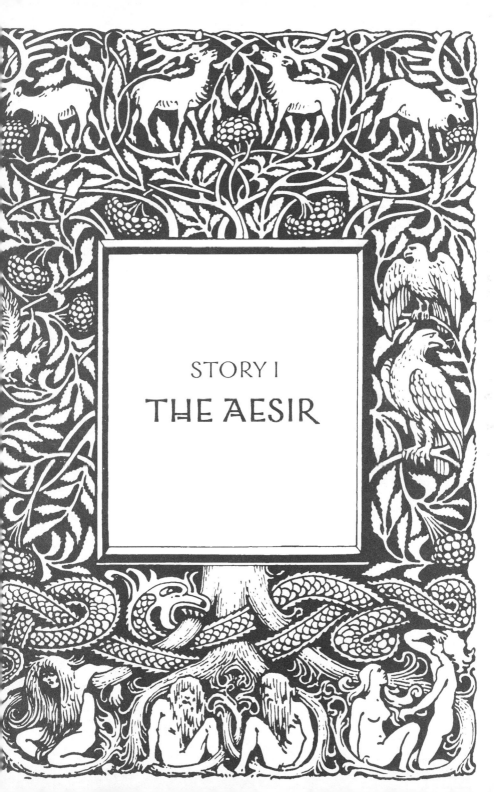

STORY I

THE ÆSIR

PART I

A Giant — A Cow — and a Hero

I n the beginning of ages there lived a cow, whose breath was sweet, and whose milk was bitter. This cow was called Audhumla, and she lived all by herself on a frosty, misty plain, where there was nothing to be seen but heaps of snow and ice piled strangely over one another. Far away to the north it was night, far away to the south it was day; but all around where Audhumla lay a cold, grey twilight reigned. By and by a giant came out of the dark north, and lay down upon the ice near Audhumla. "You must let me drink of your milk," said the giant to the cow; and though her milk was bitter, he liked it well, and for him it was certainly good enough.

After a little while the cow looked all round her for something to eat, and she saw a very few grains of salt sprinkled over the ice; so she licked the salt, and breathed with her sweet breath, and then long golden locks rose out of the ice, and the southern day shone upon them, which made them look bright and glittering.

The giant frowned when he saw the glitter of the golden hair; but Audhumla licked the pure salt again, and a head of a man rose out of the ice. The head was more handsome than could be described, and a wonderful light beamed out of its clear blue eyes. The giant frowned still more when he saw the head; but Audhumla licked the salt a third time, and then an entire man arose—a hero majestic in strength and marvellous in beauty.

Now, it happened that when the giant looked full in the face of that beautiful man, he hated him with his whole heart, and, what was still worse, he took a terrible oath, by all the snows of Ginnungagap, that he would never cease fighting until either he or Buri, the hero, should lie dead upon the ground. And he kept his vow; he did not cease fighting until Buri had fallen beneath his cruel blows. I cannot tell how it could be that one so wicked should be able to conquer one so majestic and so beautiful; but so it was, and afterwards, when the sons of the hero began to grow up, the giant and his sons fought against them too, and were very near conquering them many times.

But there was of the sons of the heroes one of very great strength and wisdom, called Odin, who, after many combats, did at last slay the great old giant, and pierced his body through with his keen spear, so that the blood swelled forth in a mighty torrent, broad and deep, and all the hideous giant brood were drowned in it excepting one, who ran away panting and afraid.

After this Odin called round him his sons, brothers, and cousins, and spoke to them thus: "Heroes, we have won a great victory; our enemies are dead, or have run away from us. We cannot stay any longer here, where there is nothing evil for us to fight against."

The heroes looked round them at the words of Odin. North, south, east, and west there was no one to fight against them anywhere, and they called out with one voice, "It is well spoken, Odin; we follow you."

"Southward," answered Odin, "heat lies, and northward night. From the dim east the sun begins his journey westward home."

"Westward home!" shouted they all; and westward they went.

Odin rode in the midst of them, and they all paid to him reverence and homage as to a king and father. On his right hand rode Thor, Odin's strong, warlike, eldest son. On his left hand rode Baldur, the most beautiful and exalted of his children; for the very light of the sun itself shone forth from his pure and noble brow. After him came Tyr the Brave; the Silent Vidar; Hödur, who, alas! was born blind; Hermod the Flying Word; Bragi, Hænir, and many more mighty lords and heroes; and then came a shell chariot, in which sat Frigga, the wife of Odin, with all her daughters, friends, and tirewomen.

Eleven months they journeyed westward, enlivening the way with cheerful songs and conversation, and at the twelfth new moon they pitched their tents upon a range of hills which stood near the borders of an inland sea. The greater part of one night they were disturbed by mysterious whisperings, which appeared to proceed from the sea-coast, and creep up the mountain side; but as Tyr, who got up half a dozen times, and ran furiously about among the gorse and bushes, always returned saying that he could see no one, Frigga and her maidens at length resigned themselves to sleep, though they certainly trembled and started a good deal at intervals. Odin lay awake all night, however; for he felt certain that something unusual was going to happen. And such proved to be the case; for in the morning, before the tents were struck, a most terrific hurricane levelled the poles, and tore in pieces the damask coverings, swept from over the water furiously up the mountain gorges, round the base of the hills, and up again all along their steep sides right in the faces of the heroes.

Thor swung himself backwards and forwards, and threw stones in every possible direction. Tyr sat down on the top of a precipice, and defied the winds to displace him; whilst Baldur vainly endeavoured to comfort his poor mother, Frigga. But Odin stepped forth calm and unruffled, spread his arms towards the sky, and called out to the spirits of the wind, "Cease, strange Vanir (for that was the name by which they were called), cease your rough play, and tell us in what manner we have offended you that you serve us thus."

The winds laughed in a whispered chorus at the words of the brave king, and, after a few low titterings, sank into silence. But each sound in dying grew into a shape: one by one the strange, loose-limbed, uncertain forms stepped forth from caves, from gorges, dropped from the tree-tops, or rose out of the grass—each wind-gust a separate Van.

Then Niörd, their leader, stood forward from the rest of them, and said, "We know, O mighty Odin, how you and your company are truly the Æsir—that is to say, the lords of the whole earth—since you slew the huge, wicked giant. We, too, are lords, not of the earth, but of the sea and air, and we thought to have had glorious sport in fighting one against another; but if such be not your pleasure, let us, instead of that, shake hands." And, as he spoke, Niörd held out his long, cold hand, which was like a windbag to the touch. Odin grasped it heartily, as did all the Æsir; for they liked the appearance of the good-natured, gusty chief, whom they begged to become one of their company, and live henceforth with them.

To this Niörd consented, whistled good-bye to his kinsfolk, and strode cheerfully along amongst his new friends. After this they journeyed on and on steadily westward until they reached the summit of a lofty mountain, called the Meeting Hill. There they all sat round in a circle, and took a general survey of the surrounding neighbourhood.

As they sat talking together Baldur looked up suddenly, and said, "Is it not strange, Father Odin, that we do not find any traces of that giant who fled from us, and who escaped drowning in his father's blood?"

"Perhaps he has fallen into Niflheim, and so perished," remarked Thor.

But Niörd pointed northward, where the troubled ocean rolled, and said, "Yonder, beyond that sea, lies the snowy region of Jötunheim. It is there the giant lives, and builds cities and castles, and brings up his children—a more hideous brood even than the old one."

"How do you know that, Niörd?" asked Odin.

"I have seen him many times," answered Niörd, "both before I came to live with you, and also since then, at night, when I have not been able to sleep, and have made little journeys to Jötunheim, to pass the time away."

"This is indeed terrible news," said Frigga; "for the giants will come again out of Jötunheim and devastate the earth."

"Not so," answered Odin, "not so, my dear Frigga; for here, upon this very hill, we will build for ourselves a city, from which we will keep guard over the poor earth, with its weak men and women, and from whence we will go forth to make war upon Jötunheim."

"That is remarkably well said, Father Odin," observed Thor, laughing amidst his red beard.

Tyr shouted, and Vidar smiled, but said nothing; and then all the Æsir set to work with their whole strength and industry to build for themselves a glorious city on the summit of the mountain. For days, and weeks, and months, and years they worked, and never wearied; so strong a purpose was in them, so determined and powerful were they to fulfil it. Even Frigga and her ladies did not disdain to fetch stones in their marble wheel-barrows, or to draw water from the well in golden buckets, and then, with delicate hands, to mix the mortar upon silver plates. And so that city rose by beautiful degrees, stone above stone, tower above tower, height above height, until it crowned the hill.

Then all the Æsir stood at a little distance, and looked at it, and sighed from their great happiness. Towering at a giddy height in the centre of the city rose Odin's seat, called Air Throne, from whence he could see over the whole earth. On one side of Air Throne stood the Palace of Friends, where Frigga was to live; on the other rose the glittering Gladsheim, a palace roofed entirely with golden shields, and whose great hall, Valhalla, had a ceiling covered with spears, benches spread with coats of mail, and five hundred and forty entrance-gates, through each of which eight hundred men might ride abreast. There was also a large iron smithy, situated on the eastern side of the city, where the Æsir might forge their arms and shape their armour. That night they all supped in Valhalla, and drank to the health of their strong, new home, "The City of Asgard," as Bragi, their chief orator, said it ought to be called.

PART II

Air Throne, the Dwarfs, and the Light Elves

In the morning Odin mounted Air Throne, and looked over the whole earth, whilst the Æsir stood all round waiting to hear what he thought about it.

"The earth is very beautiful," said Odin, from the top of his throne, "very beautiful in every part, even to the shores of the dark North Sea; but, alas! the men of the earth are puny and fearful. At this moment I see a three-headed giant striding out of Jötunheim. He throws a shepherd-boy into the sea, and puts the whole of the flock into his pocket. Now he takes them out again one by one, and cracks their bones as if they were hazel-nuts, whilst, all the time, men look on, and do nothing."

"Father," cried Thor in a rage, "last night I forged for myself a belt, a glove, and a hammer, with which three things I will go forth alone to Jötunheim."

Thor went, and Odin looked again.

"The men of the earth are idle and stupid," said Odin. "There are dwarfs and elves, who live amongst them, and play tricks which they cannot understand, and do not know how to prevent. At this moment I see a husbandman sowing grains of wheat in the furrows, whilst a dwarf runs after him, and changes them into stones. Again, I see two hideous little beings, who are holding under water the head of one, the wisest of men, until he dies; they mix his blood with honey; they have put it into three stone jars, and hidden it away."

Then Odin was very angry with the dwarfs, for he saw that they were bent on mischief; so he called to him Hermod, his Flying Word, and despatched him with a message to the dwarfs and light elves, to say that Odin sent his compliments, and would be glad to speak with them, in his palace of Gladsheim, upon a matter of some importance.

When they received Hermod's summons the dwarfs and light elves were very much surprised, not quite knowing whether to feel honoured or afraid. However, they put on their pertest manners, and went clustering after Hermod like a swarm of ladybirds.

When they were arrived in the great city they found Odin descended from his throne, and sitting with the rest of the Æsir in the Judgment Hall of Gladsheim. Hermod flew in, saluted his master, and pointed to the dwarfs and elves hanging like a cloud in the doorway to show that he had fulfilled his mission. Then Odin beckoned the little people to come forward. Cowering and whispering they peeped over one another's shoulders; now running on a little way into the hall, now back again, half curious, half afraid; and it was not until Odin had beckoned three times that they finally reached his footstool. Then Odin spoke to them in calm, low, serious tones about the wickedness of their mischievous propensities. Some, the very worst of them, only laughed in a forward, hardened manner; but a great many looked up surprised and a little pleased at the novelty of serious words; whilst the light elves all wept, for they were tender-hearted little things. At length Odin spoke to the two dwarfs by name whom he had seen drowning the wise man. "Whose blood was it," he asked, "that you mixed with honey and put into jars?"

"Oh," said the dwarfs, jumping up into the air, and clapping their hands, "that was Kvasir's blood. Don't you know who Kvasir was? He sprang up out of the peace made between the Vanir and yourselves, and has been wandering about these seven years or more; so wise he was that men thought he must be a god. Well, just now we found him lying in a meadow drowned in his own wisdom; so we mixed his blood with honey, and put it into three great jars to keep. Was not that well done, Odin?"

"Well done!" answered Odin. "Well done! You cruel, cowardly, lying dwarfs! I myself saw you kill him. For shame! for shame!" and then Odin proceeded to pass sentence upon them all. Those who had been the most wicked, he said, were to live, henceforth, a long way underground, and were to spend their time in throwing fuel upon the great earth's central fire; whilst those who had only been mischievous were to work in the gold and diamond mines, fashioning precious stones and metals. They might all come up at night, Odin said; but must vanish at the dawn. Then he waved his hand, and the dwarfs turned round, shrilly chattering, scampered down the palace-steps, out of the city, over the green fields, to their unknown, deep-buried earth-homes. But the light elves still lingered, with upturned, tearful, smiling faces, like sunshiny morning dew.

"And you," said Odin, looking them through and through with his serious eyes, "and you——"

"Oh! indeed, Odin," interrupted they, speaking all together in quick, uncertain tones; "Oh! indeed, Odin, we are not so very wicked. We have never done anybody any harm."

"Have you ever done anybody any good?" asked Odin.

"Oh! no, indeed," answered the light elves, "we have never done anything at all."

"You may go, then," said Odin, "to live amongst the flowers, and play with the wild bees and summer insects. You must, however, find something to do, or you will get to be mischievous like the dwarfs."

"If only we had any one to teach us," said the light elves, "for we are such foolish little people."

Odin looked round inquiringly upon the Æsir; but amongst them there was no teacher found for the silly little elves. Then he turned to Niörd, who nodded his head good-

Then through the clear sky two forms came floating

naturedly, and said, "Yes, yes, I will see about it;" and then he strode out of the Judgment Hall, right away through the city gates, and sat down upon the mountain's edge.

After awhile he began to whistle in a most alarming manner, louder and louder, in strong wild gusts, now advancing, now retreating; then he dropped his voice a little, lower and lower, until it became a bird-like whistle—low, soft, enticing music, like a spirit's call; and far away from the south a little fluttering answer came, sweet as the invitation itself, nearer and nearer until the two sounds dropped into one another. Then through the clear sky two forms came floating, wonderfully fair—a brother and sister—their beautiful arms twined round one another, their golden hair bathed in sunlight, and supported by the wind.

"My son and daughter," said Niörd, proudly, to the surrounding Æsir, "Frey and Freyja, Summer and Beauty, hand in hand."

When Frey and Freyja dropped upon the hill Niörd took his son by the hand, led him gracefully to the foot of the throne, and said, "Look here, dear brother Lord, what a fair young instructor I have brought for your pretty little elves."

Odin was very much pleased with the appearance of Frey; but, before constituting him king and schoolmaster of the light elves, he desired to know what his accomplishments were, and what he considered himself competent to teach.

"I am the genius of clouds and sunshine," answered Frey; and as he spoke, the essences of a hundred perfumes were exhaled from his breath. "I am the genius of clouds and sunshine, and if the light elves will have me for their king I can teach them how to burst the folded buds, to set the blossoms, to pour sweetness into the swelling fruit, to lead the bees through the honey-passages of the flowers, to make the single ear a stalk of wheat, to hatch birds' eggs, and teach the little ones to sing—all this, and much more," said Frey, "I know, and will teach them."

Then answered Odin, "It is well;" and Frey took his scholars away with him to Alfheim, which is in every beautiful place under the sun.

PART III
Niflheim

 ow, in the city of Asgard dwelt one called Loki, who, though amongst the Æsir, was not of the Æsir, but utterly unlike to them; for to do the wrong, and leave the right undone, was, night and day, this wicked Loki's one unwearied aim. How he came amongst the Æsir no one knew, nor even whence he came. Once, when Odin questioned him on the subject, Loki stoutly declared that there had been a time when he was innocent and noble-purposed like the Æsir themselves; but that, after many wanderings up and down the earth, it had been his misfortune, Loki said, to discover the half-burnt heart of a woman; "since when," continued he, "I became what you now see me, Odin." As this was too fearful a story for any one to wish to hear twice over Odin never questioned him again.

Whilst the Æsir were building their city, Loki, instead of helping them, had been continually running over to Jötunheim to make friends amongst the giants and wicked witches of the place. Now, amongst the witches there was one so fearful to behold in her sin and her cruelty, that one would have thought it impossible even for such a one as Loki to find any pleasure in her companionship: nevertheless, so it was that he married her, and they lived together a long time, making each other worse and worse out of the abundance of their own wicked hearts, and bringing up their three children to be the plague, dread, and misery of mankind. These three children were just what they might have been expected to be from their parentage and education. The eldest was Jörmungand, a monstrous serpent; the second Fenrir, most ferocious of wolves; the third was Hela, half corpse, half queen. When Loki and his witch-wife looked at their fearful progeny they thought within themselves, "What would the Æsir say if they could see?" "But they cannot see," said Loki; "and, lest they should suspect, Witch-wife, I will go back to Asgard for a little while, and salute old Father Odin bravely, as if I had no secret here." So saying, Loki wished his wife good-morning, bade her hide the children securely indoors, and set forth on the road to Asgard.

But all the time he was travelling Loki's children went on growing, and long before he had reached the lofty city Jörmungand had become so large that his mother was obliged to open the door to let his tail out. At first it hung only a little way across the road; but he grew, Oh, how fearfully Jörmungand grew! Whether it was from sudden exposure to the air, I do not know; but, in a single day he grew from one end of Jötunheim to the other, and early next morning began to shoot out in the direction of Asgard. Luckily, however, just at that moment Odin caught sight of him, when, from the top of Air Throne, the eyes of this vigilant ruler were taking their morning walk. "Now," said Odin, "it is quite clear, Frigga, that I must remain in idleness no longer at Asgard, for monsters are bred up in Jötunheim, and the earth has need of me." So saying, descending instantly from Air Throne, Odin went forth from Asgard's golden gates to tread the earth of common men, fighting to pierce through Jötunheim, and slay its monstrous sins.

In his journeyings Odin mixed freely with the people of the countries through which he passed; shared with them toil and pleasure, war and grief; taught them out of his own large experience, inspired them with his noble thoughts, and exalted them by his example. Even to the oldest he could teach much; and in the evening, when the labours of the day were ended, and the sun cast slanting rays upon the village green, it was pleasant to see the sturdy village youths grouped round that noble chief, hanging open-mouthed upon his words, as he told them of his great fight with the giant of long ago, and then pointing towards Jötunheim, explained to them how that fight was not yet over, for that giants and monsters grew round them on every side, and they, too, might do battle bravely, and be heroes and Æsir of the earth.

One evening, after thus drinking in his burning words they all trooped together to the village smithy, and Odin forged for them, all night, arms and armour, instructing them, at the same time, in their use. In the morning he said, "Farewell, children; I have further to go than you can come; but do not forget me when I am gone, nor how to fight as I have taught you. Never cease to be true and brave; never turn your arms against one another; and never turn them away from the giant and the oppressor."

Then the villagers returned to their homes and their field-labour, and Odin pressed on, through trackless uninhabited woods, up silent mountains, over the lonely ocean, until he reached that strange, mysterious meeting-place of sea and sky. There, brooding over the waters like a grey sea fog, sat Mimer, guardian of the well where wit and wisdom lie hidden.

"Mimer," said Odin, going up to him boldly, "let me drink of the waters of wisdom."

"Truly, Odin," answered Mimer, "it is a great treasure that you seek, and one which many have sought before, but who, when they knew the price of it, turned back."

Then replied Odin, "I would give my right hand for wisdom willingly."

"Nay," rejoined the remorseless Mimer, "it is not your right hand, but your right eye you must give."

Odin was very sorry when he heard the words of Mimer, and yet he did not deem the price too great; for plucking out his right eye, and casting it from him, he received in return a draught of the fathomless deep. As Odin gave back the horn into Mimer's hand he felt as if there were a fountain of wisdom springing up within him—an inward light; for which you may be sure he never grudged having given his perishable eye. Now, also, he knew what it was necessary for him to do in order to become a really noble Asa, and that was to push on to the extreme edge of the earth itself, and peep over into Niflheim. Odin knew it was precisely that he must do; and precisely that he did. Onward and northward he went over ice-bound seas, through twilight, fog, and snow, right onward in the face of winds that were like swords; until he came into the unknown land, where sobs, and sighs, and sad unfinished shapes were drifting up and down. "Then," said Odin, thoughtfully, "I have come to the end of all creation, and a little further on Niflheim must lie."

Accordingly he pushed on further and further until he reached the earth's extremist edge, where, lying down and leaning over from its last cold peak, he looked into the gulf below. It was Niflheim. At first Odin imagined that it was only empty darkness; but, after hanging there three nights and days, his eye fell on one of Yggdrasil's mighty stems. Yggdrasil was the old earth-tree, whose roots sprang far and wide, from Jötunheim, from above, and this, the oldest of the three, out of Niflheim. Odin looked long upon its time-worn, knotted fibres, and watched how they were for ever gnawed by Nidhögg the envious serpent, and his brood of poisonous diseases. Then he wondered what he should see next; and, one by one, spectres arose from Naströnd, the Shore of Corpses—arose and wandered pale, naked, nameless, and without a home. Then Odin looked down deeper into the abyss of abysses, and saw all its shapeless, nameless ills; whilst far below him, deeper than Naströnd, Yggdrasil, and Nidhögg, roared Hvergelmir, the boiling cauldron of evil. Nine nights and days this brave wise Asa hung over Niflheim pondering. More brave and more wise he turned away from it than when he came. It is true that he sighed often on his road thence to Jötunheim; but is it not always thus that wisdom and strength come to us weeping?

PART IV
The Children of Loki

hen, at length, Odin found himself in the land of giants—frost giants, mountain giants, three-headed and wolf-headed giants, monsters and iron witches of every kind—he walked straight on, without stopping to fight with any one of them, until he came to the middle of Jörmungand's body. Then he seized the monster, growing fearfully as he was all the time, and threw him headlong into the deep ocean. There Jörmungand still grew, until, encircling the whole earth, he found that his tail was growing down his throat, after which he lay quite still, binding himself together; and neither Odin nor any one else has been able to move him thence. When Odin had thus disposed of Jörmungand, henceforth called the Midgard Serpent, he went on to the house of Loki's wife. The door was thrown open, and the wicked Witch-mother sat in the entrance, whilst on one side crouched Fenrir, her ferocious wolf-son, and on the other stood Hela, most terrible of monsters and women. A crowd of giants strode after Odin, curious to obtain a glance of Loki's strange children before they should be sent away. At

Fenrir and the Witch-mother they stared with great eyes, joyfully and savagely glittering; but when he looked at Hela each giant became as pale as new snow, and cold with terror as a mountain of ice. Pale, cold, frozen, they never moved again; but a rugged chain of rocks stood behind Odin, and he looked on fearless and unchilled.

"Strange daughter of Loki," he said, speaking to Hela, "you have the head of a queen, proud forehead, and large, imperial eyes; but your heart is pulseless, and your cruel arms kill what they embrace. Without doubt you have somewhere a kingdom; not where the sun shines, and men breathe the free air, but down below in infinite depths, where bodiless spirits wander, and the cast-off corpses are cold."

Then Odin pointed downwards towards Niflheim, and Hela sank right through the earth, downward, downward, to that abyss of abysses, where she ruled over spectres, and made for herself a home called Helheim, nine lengthy kingdoms wide and deep.

After this, Odin desired Fenrir to follow him, promising that if he became tractable and obedient, and exchanged his ferocity for courage, he should not be banished as his brother and sister had been. So Fenrir followed, and Odin led the way out of Jötunheim, across the ocean, over the earth, until he came to the heavenly hills, which held up the southern sky tenderly in their glittering arms. There, half on the mountain-top and half in air, sat Heimdall, guardian of the tremulous bridge Bifröst, that arches from earth to heaven.

Heimdall was a tall, white Van, with golden teeth, and a wonderful horn, called the Giallar Horn, which he generally kept hidden under the tree Yggdrasil; but when he blew it the sound went out into all worlds.

Now, Odin had never been introduced to Heimdall—had never even seen him before; but he did not pass him by without speaking on that account. On the contrary, being altogether much struck by his appearance, he could not refrain from asking him a few questions. First, he requested to know whom he had the pleasure of addressing; secondly, who his parents were, and what his education had been;

and thirdly, how he explained his present circumstances and occupation.

"My name is Heimdall," answered the guardian of Bifröst, "and the son of nine sisters am I. Born in the beginning of time, at the boundaries of the earth, I was fed on the strength of the earth and the cold sea. My training, moreover, was so perfect, that I now need no more sleep than a bird. I can see for a hundred miles around me as well by night as by day; I can hear the grass growing and the wool on the backs of sheep. I can blow mightily my horn Giallar, and I for ever guard the tremulous bridge-head against monsters, giants, iron witches, and dwarfs."

Then asked Odin, gravely, "Is it also forbidden to the Æsir to pass this way, Heimdall? Must you guard Bifröst, also, against them?"

"Assuredly not," answered Heimdall. "All Æsir and heroes are free to tread its trembling, many-coloured pavement, and they will do well to tread it, for above the arch's summit I know that the Urda fountain springs; rises, and falls, in a perpetual glitter, and by its sacred waters the Nornir dwell— those three mysterious, mighty maidens, through whose cold fingers run the golden threads of Time."

"Enough, Heimdall," answered Odin. "Tomorrow we will come."

PART V
Bifröst, Urda, and the Norns

din departed from Heimdall, and went on his way, Fenrir obediently following, though not now much noticed by his captor, who pondered over the new wonders of which he had heard. "Bifröst, Urda, and the Norns—what can they mean?"

Thus pondering and wondering he went, ascended Asgard's Hill, walked through the golden gates of the City into the palace of Gladsheim, and into the hall Valhalla, where, just then, the Æsir and Asyniur were assembled at their evening meal. Odin sat down to the table without speaking, and, still absent and meditative, proceeded to carve the great boar, Sæhrimnir, which every evening eaten, was every morning whole again. No one thought of disturbing him by asking any questions, for they saw that something was on his mind, and the Æsir were well-bred. It is probable, therefore, that the supper would have been concluded in perfect silence if Fenrir had not poked his nose in at the doorway, just opposite to the seat of the lovely Freyja. She, genius of beauty as she was, and who had never in her whole life seen even the shadow of a wolf, covered her face with her hands, and screamed a little, which caused all the Æsir to start and turn round, in order to see what was the matter. But Odin directed a reproving glance at the ill-mannered Fenrir, and then gave orders that the wolf should be fed; "after which," concluded he, "I will relate my adventures to the assembled Æsir."

"That is all very well, Asa Odin," answered Frey; "but who, let me ask, is to undertake the office of feeding yon hideous and unmannerly animal?"

"That will I, joyfully," cried Tyr, who liked nothing better than an adventure; and then, seizing a plate of meat from the table, he ran out of the hall, followed by Fenrir, who howled, and sniffed, and jumped up at him in a most impatient, un-Æsir-like manner.

After the wolf was gone Freyja looked up again, and when Tyr was seated once more, Odin began. He told them of everything that he had seen, and done, and suffered; and, at last, of Heimdall, that strange white Van, who sat upon the heavenly hills, and spoke of Bifröst, and Urda, and the Norns. The Æsir were very silent whilst Odin spoke to them, and were deeply and strangely moved by this conclusion to his discourse.

"The Norns," repeated Frigga, "the Fountain of Urda, the golden threads of Time! Let us go, my children," she said, rising from the table, "let us go and look at these things."

But Odin advised that they should wait until the next day, as the journey to Bifröst and back again could easily be accomplished in a single morning.

Accordingly, the next day the Æsir and Asyniur all rose with the sun, and prepared to set forth. Niörd came from Noatun, the mild sea-coast, which he had made his home, and with continual gentle puffings out of his wide, breezy mouth, he made their journey to Bifröst so easy and pleasant, that they all felt a little sorry when they caught the first glitter of Heimdall's golden teeth. But Heimdall was glad to see them; glad, at least, for their sakes. He thought it would be so good for them to go and see the Norns. As far as he himself was concerned he never felt dull alone. On the top of those bright hills how many meditations he had! Looking far and wide over the earth how much he saw and heard!

Tales of Norse Mythology

"Come already!" said Heimdall to the Æsir, stretching out his long, white hands to welcome them; "come already! Ah! this is Niörd's doing. How do you do, cousin," said he; for Niörd and Heimdall were related.

"How sweet and fresh it is up here!" remarked Frigga, looking all round, and feeling that it would be polite to say something. "You are very happy, Sir," continued she, "in having always such fine scenery about you, and in being the guardian of such a bridge."

And in truth Frigga might well say "such a bridge;" for the like of it was never seen on the ground. Trembling and glittering it swung across the sky, up from the top of the mountain to the clouds, and down again into the distant sea.

"Bifröst! Bifröst!" exclaimed the Æsir, wonderingly; and Heimdall was pleased at their surprise.

"At the arch's highest point," said he, pointing upward, "rises that fountain of which I spoke. Do you wish to see it to-day?"

"That do we, indeed," cried all the Æsir in a breath. "Quick, Heimdall, and unlock the bridge's golden gate."

Then Heimdall took all his keys out, and fitted them into the diamond lock till he found the right one, and the gate flew open with a sound at the same time sad and cheerful, like the dripping of leaves after a thunder-shower.

The Æsir pressed in; but, as they passed him, Heimdall laid his hand upon Thor's shoulder, and said, "I am very sorry, Thor; but it cannot be helped. You must go to the fountain alone by another way; for you are so strong and heavy, that if you were to put your foot on Bifröst, either it would tremble in pieces beneath your weight, or take fire from the friction of your iron heels. Yonder, however, are two river-clouds, called Körmt and Ermt, through which you can wade to the Sacred Urda, and you will assuredly reach it in time, though the waters of the clouds are strong and deep."

At the words of Heimdall Thor fell back from the bridge's head, vexed and sorrowful. "Am I to be sent away, then, and have to do disagreeable things," said he, "just because I am so strong? After all, what are Urda and the Norns to me, and Körmt and Ermt? I will go back to Asgard again."

"Nay, Thor," said Odin, "I pray you, do not anything so foolish. Think again, I beseech you, what it is that we are going to see and hear. Körmt and Ermt lie before you, as Bifröst before us. It is yonder, above both, that we go. Neither can it much matter, Thor, whether we reach the Fountain of Urda over Bifröst or through the cloud."

Then Thor blushed with shame at his own weakness, which had made him regret his strength; and, without any more grumbling or hanging back, he plunged into the dreadful river-clouds, whose dark vapours closed around him and covered him. He was hidden from sight, and the Æsir went on their way over the glittering bridge.

Daintily and airily they trod over it; they swung themselves up the swinging arch; they reached its summit on a pale, bright cloud. Thor was there already waiting for them, drenched and weary, but cheerful and bold. Then, all together, they knocked at the door of the pale, bright cloud; it blew open, and they passed in. Oh! then what did they see! Looking up to an infinite height through the purple air, they saw towering above them Yggdrasil's fairest branches, leafy and of a tender green, which also stretched far and wide; but, though they looked long, the Æsir could distinguish no topmost bough, and it almost seemed to them that, from somewhere up above, this mighty earth-tree must draw another root, so firmly and so tall it grew. On one side stood the Palace of the Norns, which was so bright that it almost blinded them to look at it, and on the other the Urda fountain splashed its cool waters—rising, falling, glittering, as nothing ever glitters on this side the clouds. Two ancient swans swam under the fount, and around it sat Three. Ah! how shall I describe them—Urda, Verdandi, Skuld. They were mighty, they were wilful, and one was veiled. Sitting upon the Doomstead, they watched the water as it rose and fell, and passed golden threads from one to another. Verdandi plucked them with busy fingers from Skuld's reluctant hand, and wove them in and out quickly, almost carelessly; for some she tore and blemished, and some she cruelly spoiled. Then Urda took the woof away from her, smoothed its rough places, and covered up some of the torn, gaping holes; but

Neither of the sisters ever stopped or
grew weary of her work.

she hid away many of the bright parts, too, and then rolled it all round her great roller, Oblivion, which grew thicker and heavier every moment. And so they went on, Verdandi drawing from Skuld, and Urda from Verdandi; but whence Skuld drew her separate bright threads no one could see. She never seemed to reach the end of them, and neither of the sisters ever stopped or grew weary of her work.

The Æsir stood apart watching, and it was a great sight. They looked in the face of Urda, and fed on wisdom; they studied the countenance of Verdandi, and drank bitter strength; they glanced through the veil of Skuld, and tasted hope. At length, with full hearts, they stole away silently, one by one, out by the pale, open door, re-crossed the bridge, and stood once more by the side of Heimdall on the heavenly hills; then they went home again. Nobody spoke as they went; but ever afterwards it was an understood thing that the Æsir should fare to the Doomstead of the Nornir once in every day.

PÄRT VI

Odhærir

 ow upon a day it happened that Odin sat silent by the Well of Urda, and in the evening he mounted Air Throne with a troubled mind. All-Father could see into Dwarf Home from his high place, as well as over man's world; his keen eye pierced, also, the mountains and darkness of Jötunheim.

On this evening, a tear, the fate-sister's gift, swam across his vision, and—behold, is that an answering tear which he sees down there in Dwarf Home, large, luminous, golden, in the dark heart of the earth? "Can dwarfs weep?" exclaimed All-Father, surprised as he looked a second and a third time, and went on looking. Fialar and Galar, the cunning dwarfs who had killed Kvasir, were kneeling beside the tear. "Is it theirs?" said All-Father again, "and do they repent?" No; it was not a tear; Odin knew it at last. More precious still, it was Kvasir's blood—golden mead now, because of the honey-drops from earth's thousand bees and flowers which these thoughtless mischief-schemers, but wonder workers, had poured into it. "It is three," said Odin, "three precious draughts!—Odhærir is its name—and now the dwarfs will drink it, and the life and the light, and the sweetness of the world will be spilt, and the heart of the world will die!" But the dwarfs did not drink it; they could only sip it a little, just a drop or two at a time. The Father of Hosts watched how they were amusing themselves.

Fialar and Galar, and a whole army of the little blackfaced, crooked-limbed creatures, were tilting the big jars over to one side, whilst first one, and then another, sucked the skim of their golden sweetness, smacking their lips after it, grinning horribly, leaping up into the air with strange gestures; falling backwards with shut eyes some of them, as if asleep; tearing at the earth and the stones of their cavern homes others, like wild beasts; rolling forth beautiful, senseless, terrible words.

It was Fialar and Galar who did that; and behold, in a little while, one after another, the dwarfs gathered round them as they spoke, and listened, open-mouthed, with clenched fists, stamping, and roaring applause until at last they seized the weapons that lay near, cocked their earth caps, each alit with a coloured star, and marched in warlike fashion, led on by Fialar and Galar, straight up through their cavernous ways, to Manheim, and across it into the Frozen Land.

Giant Vafthrüdnir, that "Ancient Talker," he who sits ever in his Hall weaving new and intricate questions for the gods, saw them; and looking up towards the brooding heavens, he exchanged glances with the Father of Hosts. But the dwarfs did not come near Vafthrüdnir's Halls; they never looked aside at him, nor up to the Air Throne of the Asa; only rushed heedlessly on till they stumbled over the Giant Gilling, who was taking a nap upon the green bank of Ifing. Ifing looks a lazy stream; one can hardly see at first sight that it flows at all; but it flows, and flows quietly, unceasingly, and is so deep that neither god nor giant has ever yet been able to fathom it. It is, in fact, that stream which divides for ever the Jötuns from the gods, and of it Odin himself once said:

> "Open shall it run
> Throughout all time,
> On that stream no ice shall be."

So the dwarfs found Gilling asleep; they knew how deep Ifing was, they knew that if they could once roll the giant Gilling in there he would never get out again, and then they should have done something worth speaking about.

"I have killed a giant," each dwarf might say, and, who knows, even the Æsir might begin to feel a little afraid of them.

"It all comes from drinking Kvasir's blood," they said, and then with their thousand little swords and spears, and sticks and stones, they worked away until they had plunged the sleeping giant into the stream. All-Father's piercing eye saw it all, and how the silly dwarfs jumped and danced about afterwards, and praised themselves, and defied the whole world, gods, giants, and men.

"It is not for us," they said, "any more to run away before Skinfaxi the shining horse that draws day over Humankind, whose mane sheds light instead of dew; we will dance before him and crown ourselves with gold, as the gods and as men do every morning."

But, in the midst of all their gleeful folly, the ground they stood upon began to shake under them, and an enormous darkness grew between them and the sky. Then the dwarfs stopped their rejoicing as if a spell had fallen upon them, dropping their weapons, huddling close to one another, cowering, whispering. Giant Suttung, son of that Gilling whom they had just slain, was coming upon them in great fury to avenge his father's death. They were dreadfully frightened; Giant Gilling asleep had been easy to manage, but a giant awake, a giant angry—they were not the same dwarfs that they had seemed half an hour ago—and so it happened that they quite easily let Suttung carry them all off to a low rock in the sea which was dry just then, but would be washed over by the morning tide. "There you are," said Suttung as he threw them all down upon the rock, "and there you shall stay until the hungry grey wave comes." "But then we shall be drowned," they all screeched at once, and the seamews started from their nests ashore and swooped round the lonely rock, and screeched as well. Suttung strode back to the shore and sat on the high rocks over the seamews' nests, and poked his fingers into the nests and played with the grey-winged birds, and paddled his feet in the breakers, and laughed and echoed the dwarfs and the seamews. "Drowned, drowned, yes, then you will be drowned." Then the dwarfs whispered together and consulted, they all talked at once, and every one of them said a different thing, for they were in fact a little intoxicated still by the sips they had taken of Odhærir. At last Fialar and Galar said the same same thing over so often that the others began to listen to them. "The sky is getting quite grey," they said, "and the stars are going out, and Skinfaxi is coming, and the waves are gathering and gathering and gathering; hoarse are the voices of the Sea-King's daughters; but why do we all sit chattering here instead of getting away as we might easily do if we did but bribe the giant Suttung with a gift." "Yes, yes, yes." shouted the silly little people, "shall we give him our cap jewels, or our swords, or our pick-axes, or our lanterns, or shall we promise to make him a necklace out of the fire of the sun and the flowers of the earth, or shall we build him a ship of ships?"

"Nonsense," said Fialar and Galar; "how should a giant care for such things as these? Our swords could not help him; he does not want pick-axes nor lanterns who lives amongst the mountain snows, nor ships who can stride across the sea, nor necklaces—Bah! A giant loves life, he drinks blood, he is greedy besides and longs to taste the gold mead of the gods."

Then all the dwarfs shouted together, "Let us give him our gold mead, our wondrous drink, Odhærir, our Kvasir's blood in the three stone jars."

Odin heard from Air Throne's blue deep. He brooded over the scene. "The sweetness, and the life, and the light of the world, then," he said, "are to satiate a giant's greediness of food and blood"—and it was for mankind that he became Terror in the trembling Height. All-Father feared nothing for the gods at that time: could he not pierce into Jötunheim, and Svartheim, and Manheim alike? Suttung heard also from the Rock.—"And what may this Odhærir be worth that you boast of so much?" he shouted to the dwarfs. "Wisdom, and labour, and fire, and life, and love," said the dwarfs. "Tut,

Tales of Norse Mythology

"There you are .... and there you shall
stay until the hungry grey wave comes"

tut, tut!" answered Suttung. "Does it taste well?" "Honey and wine; like the blood of a god and the milk of the earth." Then Suttung got up slowly from the rock, pressing it down with his hands into two little dells as he rose, and strode to the island, from which he took up all the dwarfs at a grasp—they clinging to his fists and wrists like needles to a magnet; and, with one swoop, threw them ashore just as the hungry waves began to lap and wash about the dwarf's-peril. So the dwarfs jumped, and leaped, and laughed, and sang, and chattered again, and ran on before Suttung, to fetch him the golden mead, Odhærir. Three big stone jars, all full. The Spirit-mover, the Peace-offer, the Peace-kiss. Suttung lifted the lids, and looked into the jars. "It doesn't look much," he said; "and, after all, I don't know that I shall care to taste it; but I'll take the jars home to my daughter Gunnlöd, and they will make a pretty treasure for her to keep."

Odin brooded over the scene. It was a grey winter's morning in Jötunheim—ice over all the rivers, snow upon the mountains, rime-writing across the woods, weird hoar letters straggling over the bare branches of the trees, writing such as giants and gods can read, but men see it only as pearl-drops of the cold. Suttung could read it well enough as he trudged along to his Mountain Home—better than he had ever read it before; for was he not bearing upon his shoulders the wondrous Kvasir's life-giving blood, Odhærir. Odin read it, "This is ominous, Odin; this is dark. Shall the gold mead be made captive in frozen halls?" For behold, the life-tear becomes dark in the dark land, as Suttung's huge door opened to let him in, him and his treasure, and then closed upon them both. Suttung gave the mead to his daughter Gunnlöd to keep, to guard it well, and—the heart of Manheim trembled, it was empty and cold. Then Odin looked north and south and east and west, over the whole world. "Come to me," he said, and two swift-winged ravens flew towards him. It seemed as if they came out of nothing; for in a moment they were not there and they were there. Their names were Hugin and Munin, and they came from the ends of the earth, where Odin sent them every morning. Every evening he was wont to say of them,

"I fear me for Hugin,
Lest he come not back,
But much more for Munin."

Yet they never failed to come back, both of them, at the dim hour in which they recounted to the Father of Hosts the history of the day that was past, and the hope of the day that was to come. On this evening, Munin's song was so terrible that only the strength of a god could possibly have endured to its end. Hugin struck another note, profounder and sweet. Then said Odin, when cadence after cadence had filled his ears, and he had descended from Air Throne, "Night is the time for new counsels; let each one reflect until the morrow who is able to give advice helpful to the Æsir."

But when the jewelled horse ran up along the sky, from whence his mane shed light over the whole world, when giants and giantesses, and ghosts and dwarfs crouched beneath Yggdrasil's outer Root, when Heimdall ran up Bifröst and blew mightily his horn in heaven's height, there was only one found who gave counsel to Odin, and that was Odin himself. "Odhærir," he said, "which is a god-gift, must come up to men's earthly dwellings. Go forth, Hugin, go forth, Munin," said the Asa, and he also went forth alone, none knowing where he went, nor how.

So Odin journeyed for a long, long while towards Suttung's Hall, across the windy, wintry ways of Jötunheim, seeing well before him the yellow mead as he went, through rocks, and woods, and rivers, and through night itself, until at last it happened that Odin came into a meadow upon a summer morning in Giant Land. Nine slaves were mowing in the meadow, whetting some old rusty scythes which they had, working heavily, for they were senseless fellows, and the summer day grew faster upon them than their labour grew to completion. "You seem heavy-hearted," said Odin to the thralls; and they began to explain to him how rusty and old their scythes were, and that they had no whetstone to sharpen them with. Upon this Odin offered to whet their scythes for them with his whetstone: and no sooner had he done so than the scythes became so sharp that they could have cut stones as easily as grass. Instead of mowing, however, the thralls began to clamour round Odin, beseeching him to give his whetstone to them. "Give it to me! give it to me: give it to me!" cried one and another; and all the time Odin stood quietly amongst them, throwing his whetstone up in the air, and catching it as it fell. Then the thralls tried if they could catch it, leaning stupidly across one another, with their scythes in their hands. Was All-Father surprised at what happened next? He could hardly have been that; but he was sorry when, looking down as the whetstone fell, he saw all the thralls lying dead at his feet, killed by each other's sharpened weapons. "This is an Evil Land," said Odin, as he looked down on the dead thralls, "and I am a bringer of evil into it."

So he journeyed on till he came to the house of Suttung's brother, Baugi. Odin asked Baugi to give him a night's lodging, and Baugi, who knew no more than the thralls had done who this traveller was, consented, and began to talk to Odin of the trouble he was in. "This is hay harvest," he said, "as you must have seen, walking here through the meadows; and I have a mighty field to gather in, but how to do it puzzles me, because my nine slaves whom I sent out sound and well this morning, all fell dead about the middle of the day. How they managed it, I can't imagine, and it puts me out sadly, for summer days don't last long in Jötunheim." "Well," said Odin, "I'm not a bad hand at mowing, and I don't mind undertaking to do the work of nine thralls for you, Baugi, for a certain reward you may give me, if you will." "What is that?" inquired Baugi, eagerly. "A draught of that golden mead, Odhærir, which Suttung obtained from the dwarfs, and which his daughter Gunnlöd keeps for him." "Oh! that," said Baugi, "isn't so good as my homebrewed for a thirsty mower; but you shall have it. It is a bargain between us." So Odin worked for Baugi the whole summer through with the labour of nine instead of with the labour of one; and when the last field was reaped, and wintry mists were gathering, the god and the giant began to talk over their bargain again. "We will come together to Suttung's house," said Baugi, "and my brother shall give you the draught which you desire so much." But when the two came to Suttung's house, and asked him for the mead, Suttung was exceedingly angry, and would not hear a word about it from either of them. "You don't drink it yourself, brother," pleaded Baugi, "although you might do so every day if you liked, without asking anybody's leave, or doing one stroke of work for it, whilst this man has toiled night and day for nine months that he might taste it only once." "Odhærir is for us giants, nevertheless," answered Suttung, "and well does my daughter Gunnlöd guard it from dwarfs and from men, from spectres, from Asyniur, and from Æsir. Have I not sworn that so it shall be guarded by all the snows of Jötunheim, and by the stormy waves, and by the yawning chasm of the abyss?" Then Baugi knew that nothing more was to be said, and he advised Odin to go back with him at once, and drink beer. But Odin was not to be turned from his purpose so easily. "You promised me a draught of the gold mead, Baugi," he said, "and I can see it through the rock in its three treasure jars; sit down by me and look through the rock till you can see it too." So Odin and Baugi sat down together, and pierced the rock with their glances all that day until they had made a small hole in it; and at night, when Suttung was asleep, and when Gunnlöd was asleep, and whilst the gold mead shone steadily in the heart of the cave, Odin looked up towards Asgard, and said,

> *"Little get I here by silence:*
> *Of a well-assumed form I will make good use;*
> *For few things fail the wise."*

And then this strong wise Asa picked up from the ground the little, mean, wriggling form of a worm and put it on and crept noiselessly into the hole which he and Baugi had made,

> *"The giant's ways are under me,*
> *The giant's ways are over me,"*

said Odin as he wriggled through the stone, but when he had got quite through to the inner side, to Gunnlöd's room, Odin took his proper form again.

"I see her upon her golden seat," he said as he looked upon the sleeping Gunnlöd where she lay, and Odin was surprised to see a giant-maid so beautiful. Surprised and sorry. "For I must leave her weeping," he mused. "How shall she not weep, defrauded of her treasure in an Evil Land." And Odin loved and pitied the beautiful maiden so much, that he would have returned to Asgard without the mead had that been possible. Alas for Gunnlöd, it was less possible than ever since All-Father had seen her. For Gunnlöd awoke in the light of Odin's glance and trembled, she did not know why, she did not know at first that he was an Asa, but, when he asked her for her treasure she could not keep it from him, she could not have kept anything from him. She rose from her golden couch, her blue eyes melted into the tenderness of a summer sky, she undid the bars and bolts and coverings of Odhærir, which she had guarded so faithfully till then, and knelt before Odin and stretched her hands towards him and said, "Drink, for I think you are a god."

A draught, a draught, a long, deep draught, and the spirit of the Asa was shaken through its height and through its depth, and again a draught of love flowing forth to the outermost, to the abysses, and one draught again—peace—in rushing, still.

Why are you weeping so, Gunnlöd? Oh! Why do you weep? Did you not give him your whole treasure, "your fervent love, your whole soul;" you kept nothing back, and Odhærir is for ever the inheritance of the gods. The dwarfs sold it for their lives, the giantess lost it of her love, gods win it for the world.

"It is for the Æsir, it is for men," said Odin. "It is Odin's booty, it is Odin's gift;" and immediately, in haste to share it, the Asa spread eagle's wings, and flew far up, away from the barren rock, and the black, cold halls of Suttung, towards his heavenly home. Alas for Gunnlöd! she has lost her treasure and her Asa too. How cold the cavern is now in which she sits! her light is gone out; she is left alone; she is left weeping upon her golden throne. But Odin soared upwards—flew on toward Asgard, and the Æsir came crowding upon the city's jewelled walls to watch his approach. And soon they

Tales of Norse Mythology

perceived that two eagles were flying towards the city, the second pursuing the first. The pursuing eagle was Suttung, who, as soon as he found that his mead was gone, and that Odin eagle-wise had escaped his vengeance, spread also *his* eagle's wings, very strong and very swift, in pursuit. Suttung appeared to gain upon Odin. Frigga feared for her beloved. The Asyniur and the Æsir watched breathlessly. Frost giants and Storm giants came crowding up from the deeps to see. "Does Odin return amongst the gods?" they asked, "or will Suttung destroy him?" It was not possible, however, that the struggle should end in any way but one. The Divine bird dropped from the height upon his Hall— the High One's Hall—and then there burst from him such a flood of song that the widest limits of Æsir Land were overflowed—some sounds even split themselves upon the common earth. "It is Poetry herself, it is Odin's booty, it is Odin's gift. It is for the Æsir, it is for the Æsir," said a thousand and a thousand songs. "And for men," answered All-Father, with his million ringing, changing voices; "it is for men." "Such as have sufficient wit to make a right use of it," said Loki. And this was the first discordant note that troubled Asgard after Odin's return.

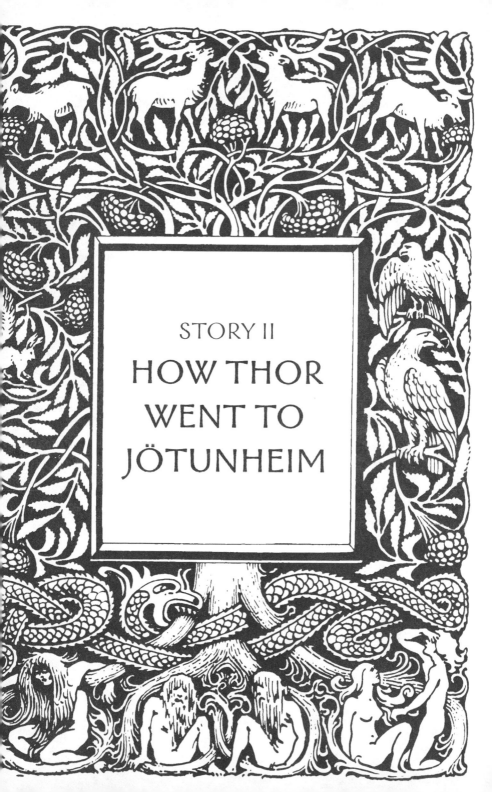

STORY II
HOW THOR WENT TO JÖTUNHEIM

PART I

From Asgard to Utgard

nce on a time, Asa Thor and Loki set out on a journey from Asgard to Jötunheim. They travelled in Thor's chariot, drawn by two milk-white goats. It was a somewhat cumbrous iron chariot, and the wheels made a rumbling noise as it moved, which sometimes startled the ladies of Asgard, and made them tremble; but Thor liked it, thought the noise sweeter than any music, and was never so happy as when he was journeying in it from one place to another.

They travelled all day, and in the evening they came to a countryman's house. It was a poor, lonely place; but Thor descended from his chariot, and determined to pass the night there. The countryman, however, had no food in his house to give these travellers; and Thor, who liked to feast himself and make every one feast with him, was obliged to kill his own two goats and serve them up for supper. He invited the countryman and his wife and children to sup with him; but before they began to eat he made one request of them.

"Do not, on any account," he said, "break or throw away any of the bones of the goats you are going to eat for supper."

"I wonder why," said the peasant's son, Thialfi, to his sister Roska. Roska could not think of any reason, and by and by Thialfi happened to have a very nice little bone given him with some marrow in it. "Certainly there can be no harm in my breaking just this one," he said to himself; "it would be such a pity to lose the marrow;" and as Asa Thor's head was turned another way, he slyly broke the bone in two, sucked the marrow, and then threw the pieces into the goats' skins, where Thor had desired that all the bones might be placed. I do not know whether Thialfi was uneasy during the night about what he had done; but in the morning he found out the reason of Asa Thor's command, and received a lesson on "wondering why," which he never forgot all his life after.

As soon as Asa Thor rose in the morning he took his hammer, Miölnir, in his hand, and held it over the goat-skins as they lay on the floor, whispering runes the while. They were dead skins with dry bones on them when he began to speak; but as he said the last word, Thialfi, who was looking curiously on, saw two live goats spring up and walk towards the chariot, as fresh and well as when they brought the chariot up to the door, Thialfi hoped. But no; one of the goats limped a little with his hind leg, and Asa Thor saw it. His brow grew dark as he looked, and for a minute Thialfi thought he would run far, far into the forest, and never come back again; but one look more at Asa Thor's face, angry as it was, made him change his mind. He thought of a better thing to do than running away. He came forward, threw himself at the Asa's feet, and, confessing what he had done, begged pardon for his disobedience. Thor listened, and the displeased look passed away from his face.

"You have done wrong, Thialfi," he said, raising him up; "but as you have confessed your fault so bravely, instead of punishing you, I will take you with me on my journey, and

Tales of Norse Mythology

teach you myself the lesson of disobedience to the Æsir which is, I see, wanted."

Roska chose to go with her brother, and from that day Thor had two faithful servants, who followed him wherever he went.

The chariot and goats were now left behind: but, with Loki and his two new followers, Thor journeyed on to the end of Manheim, over the sea, and then on, on, on in the strange, barren, misty land of Jötunheim. Sometimes they crossed great mountains; sometimes they had to make their way among torn and rugged rocks, which often, through the mist, appeared to them to wear the forms of men, and once for a whole day they traversed a thick and tangled forest. In the evening of that day, being very much tired, they saw with pleasure that they had come upon a spacious hall, of which the door, as broad as the house itself, stood wide open.

"Here we may very comfortably lodge for the night," said Thor; and they went in and looked about them.

The house appeared to be perfectly empty; there was a wide hall, and five smaller rooms opening into it. They were, however, too tired to examine it carefully, and as no inhabitants made their appearance, they ate their supper in the hall, and lay down to sleep. But they had not rested long before they were disturbed by strange noises, groanings, mutterings, and snortings, louder than any animal that they had ever seen in their lives could make. By and by the house began to shake from side to side, and it seemed as if the very earth trembled. Thor sprang up in haste, and ran to the open door; but, though he looked earnestly into the starlit forest, there was no enemy to be seen anywhere. Loki and Thialfi, after groping about for a time, found a sheltered chamber to the right, where they thought they could finish their night's rest in safety; but Thor, with Miölnir in his hand, watched at the door of the house all night. As soon as the day dawned he went out into the forest, and there, stretched on the ground close by the house, he saw a strange, uncouth, gigantic shape of a man, out of whose

 Thor fearlessly walked up to this strange monster to have a better look at him.

nostrils came a breath which swayed the trees to their very tops. There was no need to wonder any longer what the disturbing noises had been. Thor fearlessly walked up to this strange monster to have a better look at him; but at the sound of his footsteps the giant-shape rose slowly, stood up an immense height, and looked down upon Thor with two great misty eyes, like blue mountain-lakes.

"Who are you?" said Thor, standing on tiptoe, and stretching his neck to look up; "and why do you make such a noise as to prevent your neighbours from sleeping?"

"My name is Skrymir," said the giant sternly; "I need not ask yours. You are the little Asa Thor of Asgard; but pray, now, what have you done with my glove?"

As he spoke he stooped down, and picked up the hall where Thor and his companions had passed the night, and which, in truth, was nothing more than his glove, the room where Loki and Thialfi had slept being the thumb.

Thor rubbed his eyes, and felt as if he must be dreaming. Rousing himself, however, he raised Miölnir in his hand, and, trying to keep his eyes fixed on the giant's face, which seemed to be always changing, he said, "It is time that you should know, Skrymir, that I am come to Jötunheim to fight and conquer such evil giants as you are, and, little as you think me, I am ready to try my strength against yours."

"Try it, then," said the giant.

And Thor, without another word, threw Miölnir at his head.

"Ah! Ah!" said the giant; "did a leaf touch me?"

Again Thor seized Miölnir, which always returned to his hand, however far he cast it from him, and threw it with all his force.

The giant put up his hand to his forehead. "I think," he said, "that an acorn must have fallen on my head."

A third time Thor struck a blow, the heaviest that ever fell from the hand of an Asa; but this time the giant laughed out loud.

"There is surely a bird on that tree," he said, "who has let a feather fall on my face."

Then, without taking any further notice of Thor, he swung an immense wallet over his shoulder, and, turning his back upon him, struck into a path that led from the forest. When he had gone a little way he looked round, his immense face appearing less like a human countenance than some strange, uncouthly-shaped stone toppling on a mountain precipice.

"Ving-Thor," he said, "let me give you a piece of good advice before I go. When you get to Utgard don't make much of yourself. You think me a tall man, but you have taller still to see; and you yourself are a very little mannikin. Turn back home whence you came, and be satisfied to have learned something of yourself by your journey to Jötunheim."

"Mannikin or not, *that* will I never do," shouted Asa Thor after the giant. "We will meet again, and something more will we learn, or teach each other."

The giant, however, did not turn back to answer, and Thor and his companions, after looking for some time after him, resumed their journey. Before the sun was quite high in the heavens they came out of the forest, and at noon they found themselves on a vast barren plain, where stood a great city, whose walls of dark, rough stone were so high that Thor had to bend his head quite far back to see the top of them. When they approached the entrance of this city they found that the gates were closed and barred; but the space between the bars was so large that Thor passed through easily, and his companions followed him. The streets of the city were gloomy and still. They walked on for some time without meeting any one; but at length they came to a very high building, of which the gates stood open.

"Let us go in and see what is going on here," said Thor; and they went.

After crossing the threshold they found themselves in an immense banqueting hall. A table stretched from one end to the other of it; stone thrones stood round the table, and on every throne sat a giant, each one, as Thor glanced round, appearing more grim, and cold, and stony than the rest. One among them sat on a raised seat, and appeared to be the chief; so to him Thor approached and paid his greetings.

The giant chief just glanced at him, and, without rising, said, in a somewhat careless manner, "It is, I think, a foolish custom to tease tired travellers with questions about their journey. I know without asking that you, little fellow, are Asa Thor. Perhaps, however, you may be in reality taller than you appear; and as it is a rule here that no one shall sit down to table till he has performed some wonderful feat, let us hear what you and your followers are famed for, and in what way you choose to prove yourselves worthy to sit down in the company of giants."

At this speech, Loki, who had entered the hall cautiously behind Thor, pushed himself forward.

"The feat for which I am most famed," he said, "is eating, and it is one which I am just now inclined to perform with right good will. Put food before me, and let me see if any of your followers can despatch it as quickly as I can."

"The feat you speak of is one by no means to be despised," said the King, "and there is one here who would be glad to try his powers against yours. Let Logi," he said to one of his followers, "be summoned to the hall."

At this, a tall, thin, yellow-faced man approached, and a large trough of meat having been placed in the middle of the hall, Loki sat to work at one end, and Logi at the other, and they began to eat. I hope I shall never see any one eat as they ate; but the giants all turned their slow-moving eyes to watch them, and in a few minutes they met in the middle of the trough. It seemed, at first, as if they had both eaten exactly the same quantity; but, when the thing came to be examined into, it was found that Loki had, indeed, eaten up all the meat, but that Logi had also eaten the bones and the trough. Then the giants nodded their huge heads, and determined that Loki was conquered. The King now turned to Thialfi, and asked what he could do.

"I was thought swift of foot among the youth of my own country," answered Thialfi; "and I will, if you please, try to run a race with any one here."

"You have chosen a noble sport, indeed," said the King; "but you must be a good runner if you could beat him with whom I shall match you."

Then he called a slender lad, Hugi by name, and the whole company left the hall, and, going out by an opposite gate to that by which Thor had entered, they came out to an open space, which made a noble race-ground. There the goal was fixed, and Thialfi and Hugi started off together.

Thialfi ran fast—fast as the reindeer which hears the wolves howling behind; but Hugi ran so much faster that, passing the goal, he turned round, and met Thialfi half-way in the course.

"Try again, Thialfi," cried the King; and Thialfi, once more taking his place, flew along the course with feet scarcely touching the ground—swiftly as an eagle when, from his mountain-crag, he swoops on his prey in the valley; but with all his running he was still a good bow-shot from the goal when Hugi reached it.

"You are certainly a good runner," said the King; "but if you mean to win you must do a little better still than this; but perhaps you wish to surprise us all the more this third time."

The third time, however, Thialfi was wearied, and though he did his best, Hugi, having reached the goal, turned and met him not far from the starting-point.

The giants again looked at each other, and declared that there was no need of further trial, for that Thialfi was conquered.

It was now Asa Thor's turn, and all the company looked eagerly at him, while the Utgard King asked by what wonderful feat he chose to distinguish himself.

"I will try a drinking-match with any of you," Thor said, shortly; for, to tell the truth, he cared not to perform anything very worthy in the company in which he found himself.

King Utgard appeared pleased with this choice, and when the giants had resumed their seats in the hall, he ordered one of his servants to bring in his drinking-cup, called the "cup of penance," which it was his custom to make his guests drain at a draught, if they had broken any of the ancient rules of the society.

"There!" he said, handing it to Thor, "we call it well drunk if a person empties it at a single draught. Some, indeed, take two to it; but the very puniest can manage it in three."

Thor looked into the cup; it appeared to him long, but not so very large after all, and being thirsty he put it to his lips, and thought to make short work of it, and empty it at one good, hearty pull. He drank, and put the cup down again; but, instead of being empty, it was now just so full that it could be moved without danger of spilling.

"Ha! ha! You are keeping all your strength for the second pull, I see," said Utgard, looking in. Without answering, Thor lifted the cup again, and drank with all his might till his breath failed; but, when he put down the cup, the liquor had only sunk down a little from the brim.

"If you mean to take three draughts to it," said Utgard, "you are really leaving yourself a very unfair share for the last time. Look to yourself, Ving-Thor; for, if you do not acquit yourself better in other feats, we shall not think so much of you here as they say the Æsir do in Asgard."

At this speech Thor felt angry, and, seizing the cup again, he drank a third time, deeper and longer than he had yet done; but, when he looked into the cup, he saw that a very small part only of its contents had disappeared. Wearied and disappointed he put the cup down, and said he would try no more to empty it.

"It is pretty plain," said the King, looking round on the company, "that Asa Thor is by no means the kind of man we always supposed him to be."

"Nay," said Thor, "I am willing to try another feat, and you yourselves shall choose what it shall be."

"Well," said the King, "there is a game at which our children are used to play. A short time ago I dare not have named it to Asa Thor; but now I am curious to see how he will acquit himself in it. It is merely to lift my cat from the ground—a childish amusement truly."

As he spoke a large, grey cat sprang into the hall, and Thor, stooping forward, put his hand under it to lift it up.

He tried gently at first; but by degrees he put forth all his strength, tugging and straining as he had never done before; but the utmost he could do was to raise one of the cat's paws a little way from the ground.

"It is just as I thought," said King Utgard, looking round with a smile; "but we all are willing to allow that the cat is large, and Thor but a little fellow."

"Little as you think me," cried Thor, "who is there who will dare to wrestle with me in my anger?"

"In truth," said the King, "I don't think there is any one here who would choose to wrestle with you; but, if wrestle you must, I will call in that old crone Elli. She has, in her time, laid low many a better man than Asa Thor has shown himself to be."

The crone came. She was old, withered, and toothless, and Thor shrank from the thought of wrestling with her; but he had no choice. She threw her arms round him, and drew him towards the ground, and the harder he tried to free himself, the tighter grew her grasp. They struggled long. Thor strove bravely, but a strange feeling of weakness and weariness came over him, and at length he tottered and fell down on one knee before her. At this sight all the giants laughed aloud, and Utgard coming up, desired the old woman to leave the hall, and proclaimed that the trials were over. No one of his followers would *now* contend with Asa Thor, he said, and night was approaching. He then invited Thor and his companions to sit down at the table, and spend the night with him as his guests. Thor, though feeling somewhat perplexed and mortified, accepted his invitation courteously, and showed, by his agreeable behaviour during the evening, that he knew how to bear being conquered with a good grace.

In the morning, when Thor and his companions were leaving the city, the King himself accompanied them without the gates; and Thor, looking steadily at him when he turned to bid him farewell, perceived, for the first time, that he was the very same Giant Skrymir with whom he had met in the forest.

At length he tottered and fell down
on one knee before her

"Come, now, Asa Thor," said the giant with a strange sort of smile on his face, "tell me truly, before you go, how you think your journey has turned out, and whether or not I was right in saying that you would meet with better men than yourself in Jötunheim."

"I confess freely," answered Asa Thor, looking up without any false shame on his face, "that I have acquitted myself but humbly, and it grieves me; for I know that in Jötunheim henceforward it will be said that I am a man of little worth."

"By my troth! no," cried the giant, heartily. "Never should you have come into my city if I had known what a mighty man of valour you really are; and now that you are safely out of it, I will, for once, tell the truth to you, Thor. All this time I have been deceiving you by my enchantments. When you met me in the forest, and hurled Miölnir at my head, I should have been crushed by the weight of your blows had I not skilfully placed a mountain between myself and you, on which the strokes of your hammer fell, and where you cleft three deep ravines, which shall henceforth become verdant valleys. In the same manner I deceived you about the contests in which you engaged last night. When Loki and Logi sat down before the trough, Loki, indeed, eat like hunger itself; but Logi is fire, who, with eager, consuming tongue, licked up both bones and trough. Thialfi is the swiftest of mortal runners; but the slender lad, Hugi, was my thought; and what speed can ever equal his? So it was in your own trials. When you took such deep draughts from the horn, you little knew what a wonderful feat you were performing. The other end of that horn reached the ocean, and when you come to the shore you will see how far its waters have fallen away, and how much the deep sea itself has been diminished by your draught. Hereafter, men watching the going out of the tide will call it the ebb, or draught of Thor. Scarcely less wonderful was the prowess you displayed in the second trial. What appeared to you to be a cat, was, in reality, the Midgard serpent, which encircles the world. When we saw you succeed in moving it we trembled lest the very foundations of earth and sea should be shaken by your strength. Nor need you be

Tales of Norse Mythology

ashamed of having been overthrown by the old woman Elli, for she is old age; and there never has, and never will be, one whom she has not the power to lay low. We must now part, and you had better not come here again, or attempt anything further against my city; for I shall always defend it by fresh enchantments, and you will never be able to do anything against me."

At these words Thor raised Miölnir, and was about to challenge the giant to a fresh trial of strength; but, before he could speak, Utgard vanished from his sight; and, turning round to look for the city, he found that it, too, had disappeared, and that he was standing alone on a smooth, green, empty plain.

"What a fool I have been," said Asa Thor, aloud, "to allow myself to be deceived by a mountain giant!"

"Ah," answered a voice from above, "I told you, you would learn to know yourself better by your journey to Jötunheim. It is the great use of travelling."

Thor turned quickly round again, thinking to see Skrymir behind him; but, after looking on every side, he could perceive nothing, but that a high, cloud-capped mountain, which he had noticed on the horizon, appeared to have advanced to the edge of the plain.

PART II

The Serpent and the Kettle

Thor turned away from Giant-land, and on the road homeward he passed through the Sea-King's dominions. There he found that Ægir the Old was giving a banquet to all the Æsir in his wide coral-caves. At a little distance Thor stood still to listen and to look. It was a fair sight: cave within cave stretched out before him decked with choicest shells, whilst far inward lay the banqueting-hall, lighted with shining gold; white and red coral-pillars stood at uneven distances; the bright-browed Æsir reclined at the board on soft water couches; Ægir's daughters—the fair-haired waves—murmured sweet music as they waited on their guests; and little baby-ripples ran about laughing in all the corners. Thor walked through the caves and entered the hall. As he did so Odin looked up from his place at Ægir's right hand, and said, "Good evening, son Thor; how has it fared with you in Jötunheim?"

Thor's face grew a little cloudy at this question, and he only answered, "Not as it ought to have done, father." Then he placed himself amongst Ægir's guests.

"In my dominions," said King Ægir, looking all round, "an extraordinary thing has happened."

"And what may that be, brother?" asked Niörd.

"From the shores of Jötunheim," answered Ægir, "the sea has run back a quarter of a mile, drawing itself away as if a giant were drinking it in."

"Is that all you have got to say, father?" said a tall Wave, as she swept her hair over the Sea-King's shoulder, and peeped up from behind him; "is that all you know of the wonders which are going on in your deep home? Listen."

Then Ægir bent forward on his seat; the Æsir all ceased speaking, and drew in their breath; the waves raised their arched necks, and were still, listening. From a great way off came the sound of a sullen swell.

"Who is that speaking?" asked Odin.

"That is Jömungand speaking," said Thor.

"And what does he say, Thor?"

"He says that I could not conquer him."

"Pass round the foaming mead," cried Ægir, who saw that it was time to turn the conversation.

But alas! Ægir's mead-kettle was so small, that before it had gone half down the table it stood empty before Tyr.

"There is a giant called Hymir," remarked Tyr, "who lives far over the stormy waves to eastward at the end of heaven."

The Æsir all looked up.

"He has a kettle," Tyr went on to say, "which is a mile deep, and which would certainly hold mead enough for all this company."

"If Hymir would lend it to us," said Ægir, "we could finish our supper; but who would go to the end of heaven to borrow a kettle?"

Then Thor rose from the table, and began to tighten round him his belt of power; he put on his iron gloves, and took Miölnir in his hand.

"What! off again to Giant-land, Ving-Thor?" cried Ægir.

"Didn't you say you wanted Mile-deep?" said Thor. "I am going to borrow it of Hymir for you. Will you come with me, Tyr?"

Tyr sprang up joyfully, and the two brothers started on their journey. When they arrived at Hymir's dwelling, which was a roughly-hewn cavern on the shore of a frozen sea, the first person they met was a wonderful giantess with nine hundred heads, in which glittered fiery eyes, and which grew out from all parts of her body, so that it was impossible to tell whether she was walking upon her head or her heels. As Thor and Tyr were looking at her trying to discover this, a woman came out of the giant's home quite as lovely as the giantess was hideous. She greeted them on the threshold. Her golden hair fell thick upon her shoulders; her mild eyes shone upon them; and with words of welcome she held out her hands and led them into the cavern. There she offered them meat and drink, and bade them rest until her husband, Hymir, should come home. As the darkness came on, however, and the time of his expected return drew near, she became silent and anxious; and at last she said, "I am very much afraid that my husband will be angry if he sees strangers here when he comes in. Take my advice, now, Asa Thor and Asa Tyr, and hide behind one of these pillars in the rock. My lord, I assure you, is surly sometimes, and not nearly so hospitable as I could wish."

"We are not accustomed to hide ourselves," remarked Thor.

"But you shall come forth when I call you," answered the woman.

So the Æsir did as she desired. By and by they heard heavy footsteps far off, over the frozen sea, coming nearer and nearer every moment. The distant icebergs resounded, and at last Hymir burst open the door of his cavern, and stalked angrily in. He had been unsuccessful that day in the chase, his hands were frost-bitten, and a "hard-frozen wood stood upon his cheek."

As soon as the fair-browed woman saw what mood he was in she went gently towards him, placed her hand in his, and told him of the arrival of the guests; then, with a sweet smile and voice, she entreated him to receive the strangers kindly, and entertain them hospitably.

Hymir made no answer; but, at one glance of his eye towards the place where the Æsir were hidden, the pillar burst asunder, and the crossbeam which it supported fell with a crash to the ground. Eight ponderous kettles had been hanging on the beam, and all but one were shivered to atoms.

Thor and Tyr then stepped forth into the middle of the hall, and Hymir received them civilly, after which he turned his attention to supper; and, having cooked three whole oxen, he invited the Æsir to eat with him. Thor fell to work with great relish, and when he had eaten the whole of one ox, prepared to cut a slice out of another.

"You eat a great deal," said Hymir, sulkily, but Thor was still very hungry, and went on with his supper until he had eaten two entire oxen. Then said Hymir, "Another night, Ving-Thor, you must provide your own supper; for I can't undertake to keep so expensive a guest."

Accordingly, early the next morning, Hymir prepared to go out fishing, and offered Thor a place in his boat. On their way to the shore they passed a herd of oxen feeding.

"Have you provided a bait for me?" said Thor to the giant.

"You must get one for yourself," answered Hymir, surlily.

So Thor was obliged to cut off the head of one of the oxen for a bait.

"You'll never be able to carry that head," said Hymir; for, in truth, the ox to which it had belonged was an enormous animal, called "Heaven Breaking."

But Thor made nothing of the head, slung it over his shoulder, and carried it down to the boat.

As they got under way, Thor and Hymir each took an oar; but Thor pulled so fast, and with such mighty strokes, that the giant was obliged to stop for breath, and beg that they might go no further.

"We have already reached the spot," he said, "where I always catch the finest whales."

"But I want to go further out to sea," said Thor.

"That will be dangerous, Ving-Thor," said Hymir; "for if we row any further we shall come to the waters under which Jörmungand lies."

Thor laughed, and rowed on. At last he stopped, baited his hook with the ox's head, and cast the line out into the sea, whilst Hymir leant over the other side of the boat, and caught two whales.

Now, when the great Jörmungand smelt Thor's bait he opened wide his monstrous jaws, and eagerly sucked in both head, and hook, and line; but no sooner did he feel the pain than he struggled so fiercely, and plunged so wildly, that Thor's hands were in an instant dashed against the sides of the boat. Still Thor did not lose his hold, but went on pulling with such wondrous force that his feet burst through the boat, and rested on the slippery rocks beneath. At last the venomous monster's mountain-high head was hauled above the waves, and then, indeed, it was a dreadful sight to see Thor, in all the power of his god-like strength, casting his fiery looks on the serpent, and the serpent glaring upon him, and spitting forth poisoned venom. Even Hymir's sun-burnt cheek changed colour as he beheld beneath his feet the sinking boat, and at his side the deadliest monster of the deep. At last, in the wildness of his fear, he rushed before Thor, and cut his line in sunder. Immediately the serpent's head began to sink; but Thor hurled Miölnir with fearful force after it into the waters.

Then did the rocks burst; it thundered through the caverns; old mother earth all shrank; even the fishes sought the bottom of the ocean; but the serpent sank back, with a long, dull sound, beneath the waves, a deep wound in his head, and smothered vengeance in his heart.

Ill at ease and silent, Hymir then turned to go home, and Thor followed him, carrying boat and oars, and everything else, on his shoulders. Now, every fresh sight of Thor increased the giant's envy and rage; for he could not bear to think that he had shown so little courage before his brave guest, and, besides, losing his boat and getting so desperately wet in his feet by wading home through the sea, did not by any means improve his temper. When they got home, therefore, and were supping together, he began jeering and taunting Thor.

"No doubt, Asa Thor," he said, "you think yourself a good rower and a fine fisher, though you did not catch anything to-day; but can you break that drinking-cup before you, do you think?"

In the wildness of his fear, he rushed
before Thor and cut his line in sunder.

Thor seized the cup, and dashed it against an upright stone. But, lo! the stone was shattered in pieces, and the cup unbroken. Again, with greater strength, he hurled the cup against the pillars in the rock: it was still without a crack.

Now, it happened that the beautiful woman was sitting spinning at her wheel just behind where Thor was standing. From time to time she chanted snatches of old runes and sagas in soft tones; and now, when Thor stood astonished that the cup was not broken, the woman's voice fell on his ear, singing low the following words:

> *"Hard the pillar, hard the stone,*
> *Harder yet the giant's bone.*
> *Stones shall break and pillars fall;*
> *Hymir's forehead breaks them all."*

Then Thor once more took the cup, and hurled it against the giant's forehead. The cup was this time shivered to pieces; but Hymir himself was unhurt, and cried out, "Well done at last, Ving-Thor; but can you carry that mile-deep kettle out of my hall, think you?"

Tyr tried to lift it, and could not even raise the handle.

Then Thor grasped it by the rim, and, as he did so, his feet pressed through the floor. With a mighty effort he lifted it; he placed it on his head, while the rings rang at his feet; and so in triumph he bore off the kettle, and set out again for Ægir's Hall.

After journeying a little way he chanced to look round, and then he saw that a host of many-headed giants, with Hymir for their leader, were thronging after him. From every cavern, and iceberg, and jagged peak some hideous monster grinned and leered as a great wild beast waiting for his prey.

"Treachery!" cried Thor, as he raised Miölnir above his head, and hurled it three times among the giants.

In an instant they stood stiff, and cold, and dead, in rugged groups along the shore; one with his arm raised; another with his head stretched out; some upright, some crouching; each in the position he had last assumed. And there still they stand, petrified by ages into giant rocks; and, still pointing their stony fingers at each other, they tell the mighty tale of Thor's achievements, and the wondrous story of their fate.

"Pass round the foaming mead," cried King Ægir, as Thor placed "Mile-deep" on the table; and this time it happened that there was enough for every one.

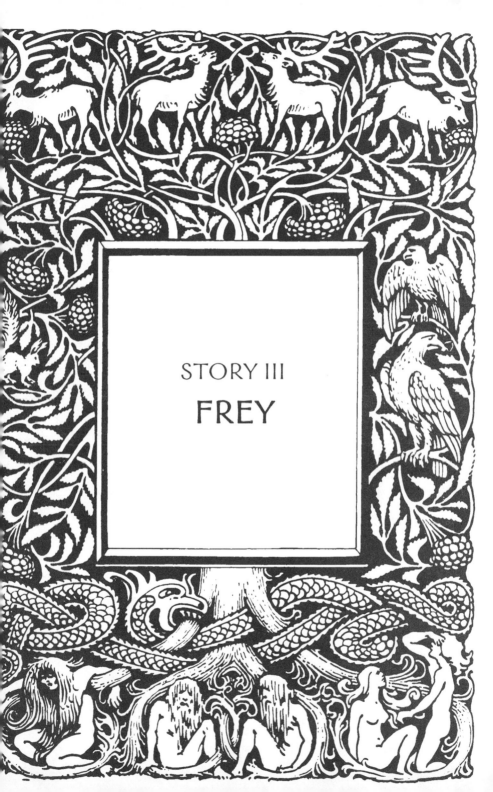

STORY III

FREY

PART I

On Tiptoe in Air Throne

 told you, some time ago, how Van Frey went away into Alfheim with the light elves, of whom Odin made him king and schoolmaster.

You have heard what Frey was like, and the kind of lessons he promised to teach his pupils, so you can imagine what pleasant times they had of it in Alfheim.

Wherever Frey came there was summer and sunshine. Flowers sprang up under his footsteps, and bright-winged insects, like flying flowers, hovered round his head. His warm breath ripened the fruit on the trees, and gave a bright yellow colour to the corn, and purple bloom to the grapes, as he passed through fields and vineyards.

When he rode along in his car, drawn by the stately boar, Golden Bristles, soft winds blew before him, filling the air with fragrance, and spreading abroad the news, "Van Frey is coming!" and every half-closed flower burst into perfect beauty, and forest, and field, and hill, flushed their richest colours to greet his presence.

Under Frey's care and instruction the pretty little light elves forgot their idle ways, and learned all the pleasant tasks he had promised to teach them. It was the prettiest possible sight to see them in the evening filling their tiny buckets, and running about among the woods and meadows to hang the dew-drops deftly on the slender tips of the grass-blades, or to drop them into the half-closed cups of the sleepy flowers. When this last of their day's tasks was over they used to cluster round their summer-king, like bees about the queen, while he told them stories about the wars between the Æsir and the giants, or of the old time when he lived alone with his father Niörd, in Noatun, and listened to the waves singing songs of far distant lands. So pleasantly did they spend their time in Alfheim.

But in the midst of all this work and play Frey had a wish in his mind, of which he could not help often talking to his clear-minded messenger and friend Skirnir. "I have seen many things," he used to say, "and travelled through many lands; but to see all the world at once, as Asa Odin does from Air Throne, that must be a splendid sight."

"Only Father Odin may sit on Air Throne," Skirnir would say; and it seemed to Frey that this answer was not so much to the purpose as his friend's sayings generally were.

At length, one very clear summer evening, when Odin was feasting with the other Æsir in Valhalla, Frey could restrain his curiosity no longer. He left Alfheim, where all the little elves were fast asleep, and, without asking any one's advice, climbed into Air Throne, and stood on tiptoe in Odin's very seat. It was a clear evening, and I had, perhaps, better not even try to tell you what Frey saw.

He looked first all round him over Manheim, where the rosy light of the set sun still lingered, and where men, and birds, and flowers were gathering themselves up for their night's repose; then he glanced towards the heavenly hills where Bifröst rested, and then towards the shadowy land which deepened down into Niflheim. At length he turned his eyes northward to the misty land of Jötunheim. There the shades of evening had already fallen; but from his high place Frey could still see distinct shapes moving about through the gloom. Strange and monstrous shapes they were, and Frey stood a little higher, on tiptoe, that he might look further after them. In this position he could just descry a tall house standing on a hill in the very middle of Jötunheim. While he looked at it a maiden came and lifted up her arms to undo the latch of the door. It was dusk in Jötunheim; but when this maiden lifted up her white arms, such a dazzling reflection came from them, that Jötunheim, and the sky, and all the sea were flooded with clear light. For a moment everything could be distinctly seen; but Frey saw nothing but the face of the maiden with the uplifted arms; and when she had entered the house and shut the door after her, and darkness fell again on earth, and sky, and sea,—darkness fell, too, upon Frey's heart.

PART II
The Gift

he next morning, when the little elves awoke up with the dawn, and came thronging round their king to receive his commands, they were surprised to see that he had changed since they last saw him.

"He has grown up in the night," they whispered one to another sorrowfully.

And in truth he was no longer so fit a teacher and playfellow for the merry little people as he had been a few hours before.

It was to no purpose that the sweet winds blew, and the flowers opened, when Frey came forth from his chamber. A bright white light still danced before him, and nothing now seemed to him worth looking at. That evening when the sun had set, and work was over, there were no stories for the light elves.

"Be still," Frey said, when they pressed round. "If you will be still and listen, there are stories enough to be heard better than mine."

I do not know whether the elves heard anything; but to Frey it seemed that flowers, and birds, and winds, and the whispering rivers, united that day in singing one song, which he never wearied of hearing.

"We are fair," they said; "but there is nothing in the whole world so fair as Gerda, the giant-maiden whom you saw last night in Jötunheim."

"Frey has dew-drops in his eyes," the little elves said to each other in whispers as they sat round looking up at him, and they felt very much surprised; for only to men and the Æsir is it permitted to be sorrowful and weep.

Soon, however, wiser people noticed the change that had come over the summer-king, and his good-natured father, Niörd, sent Skirnir one day into Alfheim to inquire into the cause of Frey's sorrow.

He found him walking alone in a shady place, and Frey was glad enough to tell his trouble to his wise friend.

When he had related the whole story, he said, "And now you will see that there is no use in asking me to be merry as I used to be; for how can I ever be happy in Alfheim, and enjoy the summer and sunshine, while my dear Gerda, whom I love, is living in a dark, cold land, among cruel giants?"

"If she be really as beautiful and beloved as you say," answered Skirnir, "she must be sadly out of place in Jötunheim. Why do not you ask her to be your wife, and live with you in Alfheim?"

"That would I only too gladly do," answered Frey; "but if I were to leave Alfheim only for a few hours, the cruel giant, Ryme, would rush in to take my place; all the labours of the year would be undone in a night, and the poor, toiling men, who are watching for the harvest, would wake some morning to find their corn-fields and orchards buried in snow."

"Well," said Skirnir, thoughtfully, "I am neither so strong nor so beautiful as you, Frey; but, if you will give me the sword that hangs by your side, I will undertake the journey to Jötunheim; and I will speak in such a way of you, and of Alfheim, to the lovely Gerda, that she will gladly leave her land and the house of her giant-father to come to you."

Now, Frey's sword was a gift, and he knew well enough that he ought not to part with it, or trust it in any hands but his own; and yet how could he expect Skirnir to risk all the dangers of Jötunheim for any less recompense than an enchanted sword? and what other hope had he of ever seeing his dear Gerda again?

He did not allow himself a moment to think of the choice he was making. He unbuckled his sword from his side and put it into Skirnir's hands; and then he turned rather pettishly away, and threw himself down on a mossy bank under a tree.

"You will be many days in travelling to Jötunheim," he said, "and all that time I shall be miserable."

Skirnir was too sensible to think this speech worth answering. He took a hasty farewell of Frey, and prepared to set off on his journey; but, before he left the hill, he chanced to see the reflection of Frey's face in a little pool of water that lay near. In spite of its sorrowful expression, it was as beautiful as the woods are in full summer, and a clever thought came into Skirnir's mind. He stooped down, without Frey's seeing him, and, with cunning touch, stole the picture out of the water; then he fastened it up carefully in his silver drinking-horn, and, hiding it in his mantle, he mounted his horse and rode towards Jötunheim, secure of succeeding in his mission, since he carried a matchless sword to conquer the giant, and a matchless picture to win the maiden.

PART III
Fairest Gerda

 told you that the house of Gymir, Gerda's father, stood in the middle of Jötunheim, so it will not be difficult for you to imagine what a toilsome and wondrous journey Skirnir had. He was a brave hero, and he rode a brave horse; but, when they came to the barrier of murky flame that surrounds Jötunheim, a shudder came over both.

"Dark it is without," said Skirnir to his horse, "and you and I must leap through flame, and go over hoar mountains among Giant Folk. The giants will take us both, or we shall return victorious together."

Then he patted his horse's neck, and touched him with his armed heel, and with one bound he cleared the barrier, and his hoofs rang on the frozen land.

Their first day's journey was through the land of the Frost Giants, whose prickly touch kills, and whose breath is sharper than swords. Then they passed through the dwellings of the horse-headed and vulture-headed giants,— monsters terrible to see. Skirnir hid his face, and the horse flew along swifter than the wind.

On the evening of the third day they reached Gymir's house. Skirnir rode round it nine times; but though there were twenty doors, he could find no entrance; for fierce three-headed dogs guarded every door-way.

At length he saw a herdsman pass near, and he rode up and asked him how it was possible for a stranger to enter Gymir's house, or get a sight of his fair daughter Gerda.

"Are you doomed to death, or are you already a dead man," answered the herdsman, "that you talk of seeing Gymir's fair daughter, or entering a house from which no one ever returns?"

"My death is fixed for one day," said Skirnir, in answer, and his voice, the voice of an Asa, sounded loud and clear through the misty air of Jötunheim. It reached the ears of the fair Gerda as she sat in her chamber with her maidens.

"What is that noise of noises," she said, "that I hear? The earth shakes with it, and all Gymir's halls tremble."

Then one of the maidens got up, and peeped out of the window.

"I see a man," she said; "he has dismounted from his horse, and he is fearlessly letting it graze before the door."

"Go out and bring him in stealthily, then," said Gerda; "I must again hear him speak; for his voice is sweeter than the ringing of bells."

So the maiden rose, and opened the house-door softly, lest the grim giant, Gymir, who was drinking mead in the banquet-hall with seven other giants, should hear and come forth.

Skirnir heard the door open, and understanding the maiden's sign, he entered with stealthy steps, and followed her to Gerda's chamber. As soon as he entered the doorway the light from her face shone upon him, and he no longer wondered that Frey had given up his sword.

"Are you the son of an Asa, or an Alf, or of a wise Van?" asked Gerda; "and why have you come through flame and snow to visit our halls?"

Then Skirnir came forward and knelt at Gerda's feet, and gave his message, and spoke as he had promised to speak of Van Frey and of Alfheim.

 He put the cup into Gerda's hand, and bade her look.

Gerda listened; and it was pleasant enough to talk to her, looking into her bright face; but she did not seem to understand much of what he said.

He promised to give her eleven golden apples from Idūna's grove if she would go with him, and that she should have the magic ring Draupnir from which every day a still fairer jewel fell. But he found there was no use in talking of beautiful things to one who had never in all her life seen anything beautiful.

Gerda smiled at him as a child smiles at a fairy tale.

At length he grew angry. "If you are so childish, maiden," he said, "that you can believe only what you have seen, and have no thought of Æsirland or the Æsir, then sorrow and utter darkness shall fall upon you; you shall live alone on the Eagle Mount turned towards Hel. Terrors shall beset you; weeping shall be your lot. Men and Æsir will hate you, and you shall be doomed to live for ever with the Frost Giant, Ryme, in whose cold arms you will wither away like a thistle on a housetop."

"Gently," said Gerda, turning away her bright head, and sighing. "How am I to blame? you make such a talk of your Æsir and your Æsir; but how can I know about it, when all my life long I have lived with giants?"

At these words, Skirnir rose as if he would have departed, but Gerda called him back.

"You must drink a cup of mead," she said, "in return for your sweet-sounding words."

Skirnir heard this gladly, for now he knew what he would do. He took the cup from her hand, drank off the mead, and, before he returned it, he contrived clearly to pour in the water from his drinking-horn, on which Frey's image was painted; then he put the cup into Gerda's hand, and bade her look.

She smiled as she looked; and the longer she looked, the sweeter grew her smile; for she looked for the first time on a face that loved her, and many things became clear to her that she had never understood before. Skirnir's words were no longer like fairy tales. She could now believe in Æsirland, and in all beautiful things.

Tales of Norse Mythology

"Go back to your master," she said, at last, "and tell him that in nine days I will meet him in the warm wood Barri."

After hearing these joyful words, Skirnir made haste to take leave, for every moment that he lingered in the giant's house he was in danger. One of Gerda's maidens conducted him to the door, and he mounted his horse again, and rode from Jötunheim with a glad heart.

PART IV
The Wood Barri

hen Skirnir got back to Alfheim, and told Gerda's answer to Frey, he was disappointed to find that his master did not immediately look as bright and happy as he expected.

"Nine days!" he said; "but how can I wait nine days? One day is long, and three days are very long, but 'nine days' might as well be a whole year."

I have heard children say such things when one tells them to wait for a new toy.

Skirnir and old Niörd only laughed at it; but Freyja and all the ladies of Asgard made a journey to Alfheim, when they heard the story, to comfort Frey, and hear all the news about the wedding.

"Dear Frey," they said, "it will never do to lie still here, sighing under a tree. You are quite mistaken about the time being long; it is hardly long enough to prepare the marriage presents, and talk over the wedding. You have no idea how busy we are going to be; everything in Alfheim will have to be altered a little."

At these words Frey really did lift up his head, and wake up from his musings. He looked, in truth, a little frightened at the thought; but, when all the Asgard ladies were ready to work for his wedding, how could he make any objection? He was not allowed to have much share in the business himself; but he had little time, during the nine days, to indulge in private thought, for never before was there such a commotion in Alfheim. The ladies found so many things that wanted overlooking, and the little light elves were not of the slightest use to any one. They forgot all their usual tasks, and went running about through groves and fields, and by the sedgy banks of rivers, peering into earth-holes, and creeping down into flower-cups and empty snail-shells, every one hoping to find a gift for Gerda.

Some stole the light from glow-worms' tails, and wove it into a necklace, and others pulled the ruby spots from cowslip leaves, to set with jewels the acorn cups that Gerda was to drink from; while the swiftest runners chased the butterflies, and pulled feathers from their wings to make fans and bonnet-plumes.

All the work was scarcely finished when the ninth day came, and Frey set out from Alfheim with all his elves, to the warm wood Barri.

The Æsir joined him on the way, and they made, together, something like a wedding procession. First came Frey in his chariot, drawn by Golden Bristles, and carrying in his hand the wedding-ring, which was none other than Draupnir, the magic ring of which so many stories are told.

Odin and Frigga followed with their wedding gift, the ship Skidbladnir, in which all the Æsir could sit and sail, though it could afterwards be folded up so small that you might carry it in your hand.

Then came Idūna, with eleven golden apples in a basket on her fair head, and then two and two all the heroes and ladies with their gifts.

All round them flocked the elves, toiling under the weight of their offerings. It took twenty little people to carry one gift, and yet there was not one so large as a baby's finger. Laughing, and singing, and dancing, they entered the warm wood, and every summer flower sent a sweet breath after them. Everything on earth smiled on the wedding-day of Frey and Gerda, only—when it was all over, and every one had gone home, and the moon shone cold into the wood—it seemed as if the Vanir spoke to one another.

"Odin," said one voice, "gave his eye for wisdom, and we have seen that it was well done."

"Frey," answered the other, "has given his sword for happiness. It may be well to be unarmed while the sun shines and bright days last; but when Ragnarök has come, and the sons of Muspell ride down to the last fight, will not Frey regret his sword?"

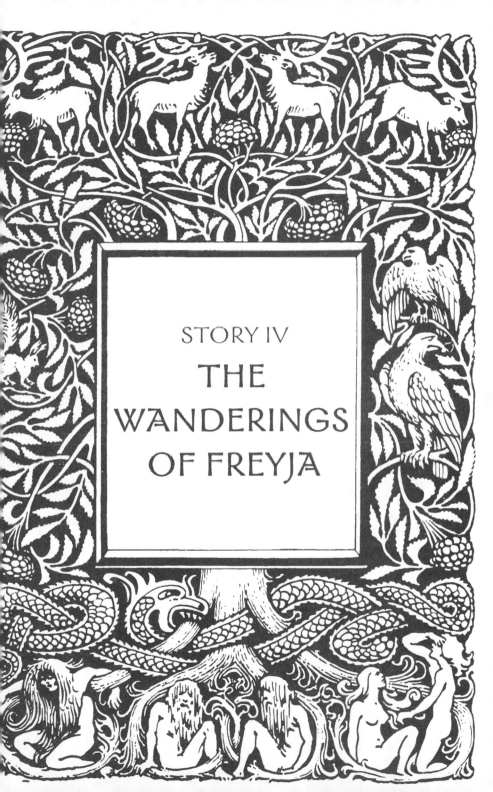

STORY IV

THE
WANDERINGS
OF FREYJA

PART I

The Necklace Brisingamen

ow, though Frey was made king and school-master of the light elves, and spent the greater part of his time with them in Alfheim, his sister Freyja remained in the city of Asgard, and had a palace built for her named Folkvang. In this palace there was one very beautiful hall, Sessrymnir—the "Roomy Seated"—where Freyja entertained her guests, and she had always plenty of them; for every one liked to look at her beautiful face, and listen to her enchanting music which was quite superior to anybody else's. She had, moreover, a wonderful husband named Odur, who was one of the sons of the immortals, and had come from a long way off on purpose to marry her. Freyja was a little proud of this, and used often to speak of it to Frigga and the other ladies of Asgard. Some of them said she was a very fortunate person; but some were a little jealous of her, whilst Frigga always gravely warned her not to be vain on account of her happiness, lest sorrow should overtake her unawares.

Everything went on quite smoothly, however, for a long time, Freyja leading a very gay and beautiful life in the sunshine of her happiness, and herself a very radiant joy to every one around her. But one day, one unlucky day, Freyja, this fair and sunshiny young Vana, went out alone from Asgard to take a walk in Alfheim. She hoped to meet somewhere thereabouts her dear brother Frey, whom she had not seen for a long time, and of whom she wanted to ask a very particular favour. The occasion for it was this;—Heimdall and Ægir were expected to dine at Valhalla the next day, and Freyja and her husband were invited to meet them. All the lords and ladies of Asgard were to be there. Niörd, too, was coming, with his new wife, Skadi, the daughter of a giant.

"Every one will be beautifully dressed," said Freyja, "and I have not a single ornament to wear."

"But you are more beautiful than any one, Freyja," said her husband; "for you were born in the spacious Wind-Home."

"All are not so high-minded as you, Odur," answered his wife; "and if I go to Valhalla without an ornament of any kind I shall certainly be looked down upon."

So saying, Freyja set off, as I told you, to Alfheim, determined to ask of her good-natured brother a garland of flowers at least. But somehow or other she could not find Frey anywhere. She tried to keep in Alfheim—she thought she was there; but all the time she was thinking of her dress and her ornaments, planning what she should wear, and her steps went downward, downward, away from Alfheim to the cavern of four dwarfs.

"Where am I?" said Freyja to herself, as she at last lost the light of day, and went down, wandering on deeper and deeper between the high walls, and under the firm roof of rock. "Why, surely this must be Svartheim; and yet it is not unpleasant, nor quite dark here, though the sun is not shining."

And in truth it was not dark; for, far on before her, winding in and out through the cavern's innermost recesses, were groups of little men, who had each a lantern in his cap and a pick-axe in his hand; and they were working hard, digging for diamonds, which they piled up the walls, and hung across the roof in white and rose-coloured coronets, marvellously glittering.

Four clever little dwarf-chiefs were there directing the labours of the rest; but, as soon as they caught sight of

Freyja, they sat down in the centre of the cavern, and began to work diligently at something which they held between them, bending over it with strange chattering and grimaces. Freyja felt very curious to see what it was; but her eyes were so dazzled with the blaze of diamonds and lanterns, that she was obliged to go nearer in order to distinguish it clearly. Accordingly, she walked on to where the four dwarfs were sitting, and peeped over their shoulders. Oh! brilliant! exquisitely worked! bewildering!

Freyja drew back again with almost blinded eyes; for she had looked upon the necklace Brisingamen, and at the same moment a passionate wish burst forth in her heart to have it for her own, to wear it in Valhalla, to wear it always round her own fair neck. "Life to me," said Freyja, "is no longer worth having without Brisingamen." Then the dwarfs held it out to her, but also looked cunningly at one another as they did so, and burst into a laugh so loud that it rang through the vaulted caverns, echoed and echoed back again from side to side, from dwarf to dwarf, from depth to depth.

Freyja, however, only turned her head a little on one side, stretched out her hand, grasped the necklace with her small fingers, and then ran out of the cavern as quickly as ever she could, up again to the green hill-side. There she sat down and fitted the brilliant ornament about her neck, after which she looked a little shyly at the reflection of herself in a still pool that was near, and turned homewards with an exulting heart. She felt certain that all was well with her; nevertheless, all was not well, but very miserable indeed. When Freyja was come back to Asgard again, and to her palace of Folkvang, she sought her own private apartments, that she might see Odur alone, and make him admire her necklace Brisingamen. But Odur was not there. She searched in every room, hither and thither; but alas! he was not to be found in any room or any hall in all the palace of Folkvang. Freyja searched for him in every place; she walked restlessly about, in and out, among the places of the "Roomy Seated." She peered wistfully, with sad eyes, in the face of every guest; but the only face she cared to see, she never saw.

 Then the dwarfs held it out to her.

Odur was gone, gone back for ever to the home of the Immortals. Brisingamen and Odur could not live together in the palace of Folkvang. But Freyja did not know this; she did not know why Odur was gone, nor where he was gone; she only saw he was not there, and she wrung her hands sadly, and watered her jewels with salt, warm tears.

As she sat thus and mourned in the entrance of her palace, all the ladies of Asgard passed by on their way to Valhalla, and looked at her. Some said one thing, some another; but no one said anything at all encouraging, or much to the purpose. Frigga passed by last of all, and she raised her head with a little severe shake, saying something about beauty, and pride, and punishment, which sank down so deeply into the heart of the sorrow-stricken young Vana that she got up with a desperate resolution, and, presenting herself before the throne of Asa Odin, spoke to him thus: "Father of Æsir, listen to my weeping, and do not turn away from me with a cruel frown. I have searched through my palace of Folkvang, and all through the city of Asgard, but nowhere is Odur the Immortal to be found. Let me go, Father Odin, I beseech you, and seek him far and near, across the earth, through the air, over the sea, even to the borders of Jötunheim."

And Odin answered, "Go, Freyja, and good fortune go with you."

Then Freyja sprang into her swift, softly-rolling chariot, which was drawn by two cats, waved her hand as she rose over the city, and was gone.

PART II

Loki — The Iron Wood — A Boundless Waste

he cats champed their bright bits, and skimmed alike over earth and air with swift, clinging steps, eager and noiseless. The chariot rolled on, and Freyja was carried away up and down into every part of the world, weeping golden tears wherever she went; they fell down from her pale cheeks, and rippled away behind her in little sunshiny rivers, that carried beauty and weeping to every land. She came to the greatest city in the world, and drove down its wide streets.

"But none of the houses here are good enough for Odur," said Freyja to herself; "I will not ask for him at such doors as these."

So she went straight on to the palace of the king.

"Is Odur in this palace?" she asked of the gate-keeper. "Is Odur, the Immortal, living with the king?"

But the gate-keeper shook his head, and assured her that his master had never even heard of such a person.

Then Freyja turned away, and knocked at many other stately doors, asking for Odur; but no one in all that great city so much as knew her husband's name.

Then Freyja went into the long, narrow lanes and shabby streets, where the poor people lived, but there it was all the same; every one said only, "No—not here," and stared at her.

In the night-time Freyja went quite away from the city, and the lanes, and the cottages, far off to the side of a lake, where she lay down and looked over into the water.

By and by the moon came and looked there too, and the Queen of Night saw a calm face in the water, serene and high; but the Queen of Beauty saw a troubled face, frail and fair.

Brisingamen was reflected in the water too, and its rare colours flashed from the little waves. Freyja was pleased at the sight of her favourite ornament, and smiled even in the midst of her tears; but as for the moon, instead of Brisingamen, the deep sky and the stars were around her.

At last Freyja slept by the side of the lake, and then a dark shape crept up the bank on which she was lying, sat down beside her, and took her fair head between its hands. It was Loki, and he began to whisper into Freyja's ear as she slept.

"You were quite right, Freyja," he said, "to go out and try to get something for yourself in Svartheim, instead of staying at home with your husband. It was very wise of you to care more for your dress and your beauty than for Odur. You went down into Svartheim, and found Brisingamen. Then the Immortal went away; but is not Brisingamen better then he? Why do you cry, Freyja? Why do you start so?"

Freyja turned, moaning, and tried to lift her head from between his hands; but she could not, and it seemed in her dream as if a terrible nightmare brooded over her.

"Brisingamen is dragging me down," she cried in her sleep, and laid her little hand upon the clasp without knowing what she was doing.

Then a great laugh burst forth in Svartheim, and came shuddering up through the vaulted caverns until it shook the ground upon which she lay. Loki started up, and was gone before Freyja had time to open her eyes.

It was morning, and the young Vana prepared to set out on her journey.

Tales of Norse Mythology

"Brisingamen is fair," she said, as she bade farewell to her image in the lake. "Brisingamen is fair; but I find it heavy sometimes."

After this, Freyja went to many cities, and towns, and villages, asking everywhere for Odur; but there was not one in all the world who could tell her where he was gone, and at last her chariot rolled eastward and northward to the very borders of Jötunheim. There Freyja stopped; for before her lay Jarnvid, the Iron Wood, which was one road from earth to the abode of the giants, and whose tall trees, black and hard, were trying to pull down the sky with their iron claws. In the entrance sat an Iron Witch, with her back to the forest and her face towards the Vana. Jarnvid was full of the sons and daughters of this Iron Witch; they were wolves, and bears, and foxes, and many-headed ravenous birds.

"Eastward," croaked a raven as Freyja drew near,

"Eastward in the Iron Wood
The old one sitteth;"

and there she did sit, talking in quarrelsome tones to her wolf-sons and vulture-daughters, who answered from the wood behind her, howling, screeching, and screaming all at the same time. There was a horrible din, and Freyja began to fear that her low voice would never be heard. She was obliged to get out of her chariot, and walk close up to the old witch, so that she might whisper in her ear.

"Can you tell me, old mother," she said, "where Odur is? Have you seen him pass this way?"

"I don't understand one word of what you are saying," answered the iron woman; "and if I did, I have no time to waste in answering foolish questions."

Now, the witch's words struck like daggers into Freyja's heart, and she was not strong enough to pull them out again; so she stood there a long time, not knowing what she should do.

"You had better go," said the crone to her at last; "there's no use in standing there crying." For this was the grandmother of strong-minded women, and she hated tears.

Then Freyja got into her chariot again, and went westward a long way to the wide, boundless land where impenetrable forests were growing, and undying nature reigned in silence. She knew that the silent Vidar was living there; for, not finding any pleasure in the gay society of Asgard, he had obtained permission from Father Odin to retire to this place. "He is one of the Æsir, and perhaps he will be able to help me," said the sad-hearted young Vana, as her chariot rolled on through empty moor-lands and forests, always in twilight. Her ear heard no sound, her eye saw no living shape; but still she went on with a trembling hope till she came to the spot

> "Begrown with branches
> And high grass,
> Which was Vidar's dwelling."

Vidar was sitting there firm as an oak, and as silent as night. Long grass grew up through his long hair, and the branches of trees crossed each other over his eyes; his ears were covered with moss, and dew-drops glistened upon his beard.

"It is almost impossible to get to him," sighed Freyja, "through all these wet leaves, and I am afraid his moss-covered ears are very deaf." But she threw herself down on the ground before him, and said, "Tell me, Vidar, does Odur hide among thick trees? or is he wandering over the broad west lands?"

Vidar did not answer her—only a pale gleam shot over his face, as if reflected from that of Freyja, like sunshine breaking through a wood.

"He does not hear me," said Freyja to herself, and she crushed nearer to him through the branches. "Only tell me, Vidar," she said, "is Odur here?" But Vidar said nothing, for he had no voice.

Then Freyja hid her face in her lap, and wept bitterly for a long time. "An Asa," she said, at last, looking up, "is no better to one than an Iron Witch when one is really in trouble;" and then she gathered her disordered dress about her, threw back her long bright hair, and, springing into her chariot, once again went wearily on her way.

"Can you tell me, old mother," she said,
  "where Odur is?"

PART III

The King of the Sea and His Daughters

t last she came to the wide sea-coast, and there everything was gloriously beautiful. It was evening, and the western sky looked like a broad crimson flower. No wind stirred the ocean, but the small waves rippled in rose-coloured froth on the shore, like the smiles of a giant at play.

Ægir, the old Sea-King, supported himself on the sand, whilst the cool waters were laving his breast, and his ears drank their sweet murmur; for nine waves were his beautiful daughters, and they and their father were talking together. Now, though Ægir looked so stormy and old he was really as gentle as a child, and no mischief would ever have happened in his kingdom if he had been left to himself. But he had a cruel wife, called Ran, who was the daughter of a giant, and so eagerly fond of fishing that, whenever any of the rough winds came to call upon her husband, she used to steal out of the deep sea-caves where she lived, and follow ships for miles under the water, dragging her net after her, so that she might catch anyone who fell overboard.

Freyja wandered along the shore towards the place where the Sea-King was lying, and as she went she heard him speaking to his daughters.

"What is the history of Freyja?" he asked.

And the first wave answered, "Freyja is a fair young Vana, who once was happy in Asgard."

Then the second wave said, "But she left her fair palace there, and Odur, her Immortal Love."

Third wave, "She went down to the cavern of dwarfs."

Fourth wave, "She found Brisingamen there, and carried it away with her."

Fifth wave, "But when she got back to Folkvang she found that Odur was gone."

Sixth wave, "Because the Vana had loved herself more than Immortal Love."

Seventh wave, "Freyja will never be happy again, for Odur will never come back."

Eighth wave, "Odur will never come back as long as the world shall last."

Ninth wave, "Odur will never return, nor Freyja forget to weep."

Freyja stood still, spell-bound, listening, and when she heard the last words, that Odur would never come back, she wrung her hands, and cried, "O, Father Ægir! trouble comes, comes surging up from a wide sea, wave over wave, into my soul."

And in truth it seemed as if her words had power to change the whole surface of the ocean—wave over wave rose higher and spoke louder—Ran was seen dragging her net in the distance—old Ægir shouted, and dashed into the deep—sea and sky mixed in confusion, and night fell upon the storm. Then Freyja sank down exhausted on the sand, where she lay until her kind daughter, the sleepy little Siofna, came and carried her home again in her arms. After this the beautiful Vana lived in her palace of Folkvang, with friends and sisters, Æsir and Asyniur, but Odur did not return, nor Freyja forget to weep.

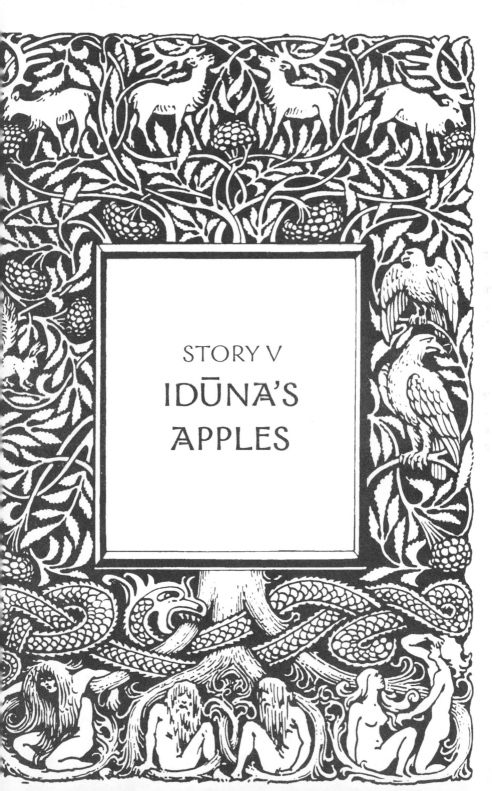

STORY V
IDŪNĀ'S
APPLES

PART I

Reflections in the Water

f all the groves and gardens round the city of Asgard—and they were many and beautiful—there was none so beautiful as the one where Idūna, the wife of Bragi, lived. It stood on the south side of the hill, not far from Gladsheim, and it was called "Always Young," because nothing that grew there could ever decay, or become the least bit older than it was on the day when Idūna entered it. The trees wore always a tender, light green colour, as the hedges do in spring. The flowers were mostly half-opened, and every blade of grass bore always a trembling, glittering drop of early dew. Brisk little winds wandered about the grove, making the leaves dance from morning till night and swaying backwards and forwards the heads of the flowers.

"Blow away!" said the leaves to the wind, "for we shall never be tired."

"And you will never be old," said the winds in answer. And then the birds took up the chorus and sang, "Never tired and never old."

Idūna, the mistress of the grove, was fit to live among young birds, and tender leaves, and spring flowers. She was so fair that when she bent over the river to entice her swans to come to her, even the stupid fish stood still in the water, afraid to destroy so beautiful an image by swimming over it; and when she held out her hand with bread for the swans to eat, you would not have known it from a water-lily—it was so wonderfully white.

Idūna never left her grove even to pay a visit to her nearest neighbour, and yet she did not lead by any means a dull life; for, besides having the company of her husband, Bragi, who must have been an entertaining person to live with; for he is said to have known a story which never came to an end, and yet which never grew wearisome. All the heroes of Asgard made a point of coming to call upon her every day. It was natural enough that they should like to visit so beautiful a grove and so fair a lady; and yet, to confess the truth, it was not quite to see either the grove or Idūna that they came.

Idūna herself was well aware of this, and when her visitors had chatted a short time with her, she never failed to bring out from the innermost recess of her bower a certain golden casket, and to request, as a favour, that her guests would not think of going away till they had tasted her apples, which, she flattered herself, had a better flavour than any other fruit in the world.

It would have been quite unlike a hero of Asgard to have refused such courtesy; and, besides, Idūna was not as far wrong about her apples as hostesses generally are, when they boast of the good things on their tables.

There is no doubt her apples had a peculiar flavour; and if any one of the heroes happened to be a little tired, or a little out of spirits, or a little cross, when he came into the bower, it always followed that, as soon as he had eaten one apple, he found himself as fresh, and vigorous, and happy as he had ever been in his life.

So fond were the heroes of these apples, and so necessary did they think them to their daily comfort, that they never went on a journey without requesting Idūna to give them one or two, to fortify them against the fatigues of the way.

Idūna had no difficulty in complying with this request; she had no fear of her store ever failing, for as surely as she took an apple from her casket another fell in; but where it came from Idūna could never discover. She never saw it till it was close to the bottom of the casket; but she always heard the sweet tinkling sound it made when it touched the golden rim. It was as good as play to Idūna to stand by her casket, taking the apples out, and watching the fresh rosy ones come tumbling in, without knowing who threw them.

One spring morning Idūna was very busy taking apples out of her casket; for several of the heroes were taking advantage of the fine weather to journey out into the world. Bragi was going from home for a time; perhaps he was tired of telling his story only to Idūna, and perhaps she was beginning to know it by heart; and Odin, Loki, and Hœnir had agreed to take a little tour in the direction of Jötunheim, just to see if any entertaining adventure would befall them. When they had all received their apples, and taken a tender farewell of Idūna, the grove—green and fair as it was— looked, perhaps, a little solitary.

Idūna stood by her fountain, watching the bright water as it danced up into the air and quivered, and turned, and fell back, making a hundred little flashing circles in the river; and then she grew tired, for once, of the light and the noise, and wandered down to a still place, where the river was shaded by low bushes on each side, and reflected clearly the blue sky overhead.

Idūna sat down and looked into the deep water. Besides her own fair face there were little, wandering, white clouds to be seen reflected there. She counted them as they sailed past. At length a strange form was reflected up to her from the water—large, dark, lowering wings, pointed claws, a head with fierce eyes—looking at her.

Idūna started and raised her head. It was above as well as below; the same wings—the same eyes—the same head— looking down from the blue sky, as well as up from the water. Such a sight had never been seen near Asgard before; and, while Idūna looked, the thing waved its wings, and went up, up, up, till it lessened to a dark spot in the clouds and on the river.

It was no longer terrible to look at; but, as it shook its wings a number of little black feathers fell from them, and flew down towards the grove. As they neared the trees, they no longer looked like feathers—each had two independent wings and a head of its own; they were, in fact, a swarm of Nervous Apprehensions; troublesome little insects enough, and well-known elsewhere, but which now, for the first time, found their way into the grove.

Idūna ran away from them; she shook them off; she fought quite bravely against them; but they are by no means easy to get rid of; and when, at last, one crept within the folds of her dress, and twisted itself down to her heart, a new, strange feeling thrilled there—a feeling never yet known to any dweller in Asgard. Idūna did not know what to make of it.

PART II

The Winged Giant

n the meantime Odin, Loki, and Hœnir proceeded on their journey. They were not bound on any particular quest. They strayed hither and thither that Odin might see that things were going on well in the world, and his subjects comporting themselves in a becoming manner. Every now and then they halted while Odin inspected the thatching of a barn, or stood at the smithy to see how the smith wielded his hammer, or in a furrow to observe if the ploughman guided his plough-share evenly through the soil. "Well done," he said if the workman was working with all his might; and he turned away, leaving something behind him, a straw in the barn, a piece of old iron at the forge-door, a grain in the furrow—nothing to look at; but ever after the barn was always full, the forge-fire never went out, the field yielded bountifully.

Towards noon the Æsir reached a shady valley, and, feeling tired and hungry, Odin proposed to sit down under a tree, and while he rested and studied a book of runes which he had with him, he requested Loki and Hœnir to prepare some dinner.

"I will undertake the meat and the fire," said Hœnir; "you, Loki, will like nothing better than foraging about for what good things you can pick up."

"That is precisely what I mean to do," said Loki. "There is a farm-house near here, from which I can perceive a savoury smell. It will be strange, with my cunning, if I do not contrive to have the best of all the dishes under this tree before your fire is burnt up."

As Loki spoke he turned a stone in his hand, and immediately he assumed the shape of a large black cat. In this form he stole in at the kitchen-window of a farm-house, where a busy housewife was intent on taking pies and cakes from a deep oven, and ranging them on a dresser under the window. Loki watched his opportunity, and whenever the mistress's back was turned he whisked a cake or a pie out of the window.

"One, two, three. Why, there are fewer every time I bring a fresh one from the oven!" cried the bewildered housewife. "It's that thieving cat. I see the end of her tail on the window-sill." Out of the window leant the housewife to throw a stone at the cat, but she could see nothing but a thin cow trespassing in her garden; and when she ran out with a stick to drive away the cow, it, too, had vanished, and an old raven, with six young ones, was flying over the garden-hedge.

The raven was Loki, the little ones were the pies; and when he reached the valley, and changed himself and them into their proper shapes, he had a hearty laugh at his own cleverness, and at the old woman's dismay.

"Well done, Loki, king of thieves," said a chorus of foxes, who peeped out of their holes to see the only one of the Æsir whose conduct they could appreciate; but Odin, when he heard of it, was very far from thinking it well done. He was extremely displeased with Loki for having disgraced himself by such mean tricks.

"It is true," he said, "that my subjects may well be glad to furnish me with all I require, but it should be done knowingly. Return to the farm-house, and place these three black stones on the table from whence you stole the provisions."

Loki—unwilling as he was to do anything he believed likely to bring good to others—was obliged to obey. He made himself into the shape of a white owl, flew once more through the window, and dropped the stones out of his beak; they sank deep into the table, and looked like three black stains on the white deal-board.

From that time the housewife led an easy life; there was no need for her to grind corn, or mix dough, or prepare meat. Let her enter her kitchen at what time of day she would, stores of provisions stood smoking hot on the table. She kept her own counsel about it, and enjoyed the reputation of being the most economical house-keeper in the whole countryside; but one thing disturbed her mind, and prevented her thoroughly enjoying the envy and wonder of the neighbouring wives. All the rubbing, and brushing, and cleaning in the world would not remove the three black stains from her kitchen table, and as she had no cooking to do, she spent the greater part of her time in looking at them.

"If they were but gone," she said, a hundred times every day, "I should be content; but how is one to enjoy one's life when one cannot rub the stains off one's own table?"

Perhaps Loki foresaw how the good wife would use her gift; for he came back from the farm-house in the best spirits. "We will now, with Father Odin's permission, sit down to dinner," he said; "for surely, brother Hœnir, while I have been making so many journeys to and fro, you have been doing something with that fire which I see blazing so fiercely, and with that old iron pot smoking over it."

"The meat will be by this time ready, no doubt," said Hœnir. "I killed a wild ox while you were away, and part of it has been now for some time stewing in the pot."

The Æsir now seated themselves near the fire, and Hœnir lifted up the lid of the pot. A thick steam rose up from it; but when he took out the meat it was as red and uncooked as when he first put it into the pot.

"Patience," said Hœnir; and Odin again took out his book of runes. Another hour passed, and Hœnir again took off the lid, and looked at the meat; but it was in precisely the same state as before. This happened several times, and even the cunning Loki was puzzled; when, suddenly, a strange noise was heard coming from a tree near, and, looking up, they saw an enormous human-headed eagle seated on one of the branches, and looking at them with two fierce eyes. While they looked it spoke.

"Give me my share of the feast," it said, "and the meat shall presently be done."

"Come down and take it—it lies before you," said Loki, while Odin looked on with thoughtful eyes; for he saw plainly that it was no mortal bird who had the boldness to claim a share in the Æsir's food.

Undaunted by Odin's majestic looks, the eagle flew down, and, seizing a large piece of meat, was going to fly away with it, when Loki, thinking he had now got the bird in his power, took up a stick that lay near, and struck a hard blow on the eagle's back. The stick made a ringing sound as it fell; but, when Loki tried to draw it back, he found that it stuck with extraordinary force to the eagle's back; neither could he withdraw his own hands from the other end.

Something like a laugh came from the creature's half-human, half-bird-like mouth; and then it spread its dark wings and rose up into the air, dragging Loki after.

"It is as I thought," said Odin, as he saw the eagle's enormous bulk brought out against the sky; "it is Thiassi, the strongest giant in Jötunheim, who has presumed to show himself in our presence. Loki has only received the reward of his treachery, and it would ill-become us to interfere in his behalf; but, as the monster is near, it will be well for us to return to Asgard, lest any misfortune should befall the city in our absence."

While Odin spoke, the winged creature had risen up so high as to be invisible even to the eyes of the Æsir; and, during their return to Asgard, he did not again appear before them; but, as they approached the gates of the city, they were surprised to see Loki coming to meet them. He had a crest-fallen and bewildered look; and when they questioned him as to what had happened to him since they parted in such a strange way, he declared himself to be quite unable to give any further account of his adventures than that he

 It spread its dark wings and rose up
into the air, dragging Loki after.

had been carried rapidly through the air by the giant, and, at last, thrown down from a great height near the place where the Æsir met him.

Odin looked steadfastly at him as he spoke, but he forbore to question him further: for he knew well that there was no hope of hearing the truth from Loki, and he kept within his own mind the conviction he felt that some disastrous result must follow a meeting between two such evil-doers as Loki and the giant Thiassi.

That evening, when the Æsir were all feasting and telling stories to each other in the great hall of Valhalla, Loki stole out from Gladsheim, and went alone to visit Idūna in her grove. It was a still, bright evening. The leaves of the trees moved softly up and down, whispering sweet words to each other; the flowers, with half-shut eyes, nodded sleepily to their own reflections in the water, and Idūna sat by the fountain, with her head resting in one hand, thinking of pleasant things.

"It is all very well," thought Loki; "but I am not the happier because people can here live such pleasant lives. It does not do me any good, or cure the pain I have had so long in my heart."

Loki's long shadow—for the sun was setting—fell on the water as he approached, and made Idūna start. She remembered the sight that had disturbed her so much in the morning; but when she saw only Loki, she looked up and smiled kindly; for he had often accompanied the other Æsir in their visits to her grove.

"I am wearied with a long journey," said Loki abruptly, "and I would eat one of your apples to refresh me after my fatigue." The casket stood by Idūna's side, and she immediately put in her hand and gave Loki an apple. To her surprise, instead of thanking her warmly, or beginning to eat it, he turned it round and round in his hand with a contemptuous air.

"It is true then," he said, after looking intently at the apple for some time, "your apples are but small and withered in comparison. I was unwilling to believe it at first, but now I can doubt no longer."

"Small and withered!" said Idūna, rising hastily. "Nay, Asa Odin himself, who has traversed the whole world, assures me that he has never seen any to be compared to them."

"That will never be said again," returned Loki; "for this very afternoon I have discovered a tree, in a grove not far from Asgard, on which grow apples so beautiful that no one who has seen them will ever care again for yours."

"I do not wish to see or hear of them," said Idūna, trying to turn away with an indifferent air; but Loki followed her, and continued to speak more and more strongly of the beauty of this new fruit, hinting that Idūna would be sorry that she had refused to listen when she found all her guests deserting her for the new grove, and when even Bragi began to think lightly of her and of her gifts. At this Idūna sighed, and Loki came up close to her, and whispered in her ear, "It is but a short way from Asgard, and the sun has not yet set. Come out with me, and, before any one else has seen the apples, you shall gather them, and put them in your casket, and no woman shall ever have it in her power to boast that she can feast the Æsir more sumptuously than Idūna."

Now Idūna had often been cautioned by her husband never to let anything tempt her to leave the grove, and she had always been so happy here, that she thought there was no use in his telling her the same thing so often over; but now her mind was so full of the wonderfully beautiful fruit, and she felt such a burning wish to get it for herself, that she quite forgot her husband's commands.

"It is only a little way," she said to herself; "there can be no harm in going out just this once;" and, as Loki went on urging her, she took up her casket from the ground hastily, and begged him to show her the way to this other grove. Loki walked very quickly, and Idūna had not time to collect her thoughts before she found herself at the entrance of Always Young. At the gate she would gladly have stopped a minute to take breath; but Loki took hold of her hand, and forced her to pass through, though, at the very moment of passing, she half drew back; for it seemed to her as if all the trees in the grove suddenly called out in alarm, "Come back, come back, Oh, come back, Idūna!" She half drew back her hand, but it was too late; the gate fell behind her, and she and Loki stood together without the grove.

The trees rose up between them and the setting sun, and cast a deep shadow on the place where they stood; a cold, night air blew on Idūna's cheek, and made her shiver.

"Let us hasten on," she said to Loki; "let us hasten on, and soon come back again."

But Loki was not looking on, he was looking up. Idūna raised her eyes in the direction of his, and her heart died within her; for there, high up over her head, just as she had seen it in the morning, hung the lowering, dark wings—the sharp talons—the fierce head, looking at her. For one moment it stood still above her head, and then lower, lower, lower, the huge shadow fell; and, before Idūna found breath to speak, the dark wings were folded round her, and she was borne high up in the air, northwards, towards the grey mist that hangs over Jötunheim. Loki watched till she was out of sight, and then returned to Asgard. The presence of the giant was no wonder to him; for he had, in truth, purchased his own release by promising to deliver up Idūna and her casket into his power; but, as he returned alone through the grove, a foreboding fear pressed on his mind.

"If it should be true," he thought, "that Idūna's apples have the wonderful power Odin attributes to them! if I among the rest should suffer from the loss!"

Occupied with these thoughts, he passed quickly among the trees, keeping his eyes resolutely fixed on the ground. He dare not trust himself to look around; for once, when he had raised his head, he fancied that, gliding through the brushwood, he had seen the dark robes and pale face of his daughter Hela.

PART III

Hela

hen it was known that Idūna had disappeared from her grove, there were many sorrowful faces in Asgard, and anxious voices were heard inquiring for her. Loki walked about with as grave a face, and asked as many questions, as any one else; but he had a secret fear that became stronger every day, that now, at last, the consequence of his evil ways would find him out.

Days passed on, and the looks of care, instead of wearing away, deepened on the faces of the Æsir. They met, and looked at each other, and turned away sighing; each saw that some strange change was creeping over all the others, and none liked to be the first to speak of it. It came on very gradually—a little change every day, and no day ever passing without the change. The leaves of the trees in Idūna's grove deepened in colour. They first became a sombre green, then a glowing red, and, at last, a pale brown; and when the brisk winds came and blew them about, they moved every day more languidly.

"Let us alone," they said at length. "We are tired, tired, tired."

The winds, surprised, carried the new sound to Gladsheim, and whispered it all round the banquet-hall where the Æsir sat, and then they rushed back again, and blew all through the grove.

"We are tired," said the leaves again; "we are tired, we are old; we are going to die;" and at the word they broke from the trees one by one, and fluttered to the ground, glad to rest anywhere; and the winds, having nothing else to do, went back to Gladsheim with the last strange word they had learned.

The Æsir were all assembled in Valhalla; but there were no stories told, and no songs sung. No one spoke much but Loki, and he was that day in a talking humour. He moved from one to another, whispering an unwelcome word in every ear.

"Have you noticed your mother Frigga?" he said to Baldur. "Do you see how white her hair is growing, and what a number of deep lines are printed on her face?"

Then he turned to Frey. "Look at your sister Freyja and your friend Baldur," he said, "as they sit opposite to us. What a change has come over them lately! Who would think that that pale man and that faded woman were Baldur the beautiful and Freyja the fair?"

"You are tired—you are old—you are going to die," moaned the winds, wandering all round the great halls, and coming in and out of the hundred door-ways, and all the Æsir looked up at the sad sound. Then they saw, for the first time, that a new guest had seated herself that day at the table of the Æsir. There could be no question of her fitness on the score of royalty, for a crown rested on her brow, and in her hand she held a sceptre; but the fingers that grasped the sceptre were white and fleshless, and under the crown looked the threatening face of Hela, half corpse, half queen.

A great fear fell on all the Æsir as they looked, and only Odin found voice to speak to her. "Dreadful daughter of Loki!" he said, "by what warrant do you dare to leave the kingdom where I permit you to reign, and come to take your place among the Æsir, who are no mates for such as you?"

Then Hela raised her bony finger, and pointed, one by one, to the guests that sat round. "White hair," she said, "wrinkled faces, weary limbs, dull eyes—these are the warrants which have summoned me from the land of shadows to sit among the Æsir. I have come to claim you, by these signs, as my future guests, and to tell you that I am preparing a place for you in my kingdom."

At every word she spoke a gust of icy wind came from her mouth and froze the blood in the listeners' veins. If she had stayed a moment longer they would have stiffened into stone; but when she had spoken thus, she rose and left the hall, and the sighing winds went out with her.

Then, after a long silence, Bragi stood up and spoke. "Æsir," he said, "We are to blame. It is now many months since Idūna was carried away from us; we have mourned for her, but we have not yet avenged her loss. Since she left us a strange weariness and despair have come over us, and we sit looking on each other as if we had ceased to be warriors and Æsir. It is plain that, unless Idūna returns, we are lost. Let two of us journey to the Urda fount, which we have so long neglected to visit, and inquire of her from the Norns—for they know all things—and then, when we have learnt where she is, we will fight for her liberty, if need be, till we die; for that will be an end more fitting for us than to sit here and wither away under the breath of Hela."

At these words of Bragi the Æsir felt a revival of their old strength and courage. Odin approved of Bragi's proposal, and decreed that he and Baldur should undertake the journey to the dwelling-place of the Norns. That very evening they set forth; for Hela's visit showed them that they had no time to lose.

It was a weary time to the dwellers in Asgard while they were absent. Two new citizens had taken up their abode in the city, Age and Pain. They walked the streets hand-in-hand, and there was no use in shutting the doors against them; for however closely the entrance was barred, the dwellers in the houses felt them as they passed.

PART IV
Through Flood and Fire

t length, Baldur and Bragi returned with the answer of the Norns, couched in mystic words, which Odin alone could understand. It revealed Loki's treacherous conduct to the Æsir, and declared that Idūna could only be brought back by Loki, who must go in search of her, clothed in Freyja's garments of falcon feathers.

Loki was very unwilling to venture on such a search; but Thor threatened him with instant death if he refused to obey Odin's commands, or failed to bring back Idūna; and, for his own safety he was obliged to allow Freyja to fasten the falcon wings to his shoulders, and to set off towards Thiassi's castle in Jötunheim, where he well knew that Idūna was imprisoned.

It was called a castle; but it was, in reality, a hollow in a dark rock; the sea broke against two sides of it; and, above, the sea-birds clamoured day and night.

There the giant had taken Idūna on the night on which she had left her grove; and, fearing lest Odin should spy her from Air Throne, he had shut her up in a gloomy chamber, and strictly forbidden her ever to come out. It was hard to be shut up from the fresh air and sunshine; and yet, perhaps, it was safer for Idūna than if she had been allowed to wander about Jötunheim, and see the monstrous sights that would have met her there.

She saw nothing but Thiassi himself and his servants, whom he had commanded to attend upon her; and they, being curious to see a stranger from a distant land, came in and out many times every day.

They were fair, Idūna saw—fair and smiling; and, at first, it relieved her to see such pleasant faces round her, when she had expected something horrible.

"Pity me!" she used to say to them; "pity me! I have been torn away from my home and my husband, and I see no hope of ever getting back." And she looked earnestly at them; but their pleasant faces never changed, and there was always—however bitterly Idūna might be weeping—the same smile on their lips.

At length Idūna, looking more narrowly at them, saw, when they turned their backs to her, that they were hollow behind; they were, in truth, Ellewomen, who have no hearts, and can never pity any one.

After Idūna saw this she looked no more at their smiling faces, but turned away her head and wept silently. It is very sad to live among Ellewomen when one is in trouble.

Every day the giant came and thundered at Idūna's door. "Have you made up your mind yet," he used to say, "to give me the apples? Something dreadful will happen to you if you take much longer to think of it." Idūna trembled very much every day, but still she had strength to say, "No;" for she knew that the most dreadful thing would be for her to give to a wicked giant the gifts that had been entrusted to her for the use of the Æsir. The giant would have taken the apples by force if he could; but, whenever he put his hand into the casket, the fruit slipped from beneath his fingers, shrivelled into the size of a pea, and hid itself in crevices of the casket where his great fingers could not come—only when Idūna's little white hand touched it, it swelled again to its own size, and this she would never do while the giant was with her.

Tales of Norse Mythology

So the days passed on, and Idūna would have died of grief among the smiling Ellewomen if it had not been for the moaning sound of the sea and the wild cry of the birds; "for, however others may smile, these pity me," she used to say, and it was like music to her.

One morning when she knew that the giant had gone out, and when the Ellewomen had left her alone, she stood for a long time at her window by the sea, watching the mermaids floating up and down on the waves, and looking at heaven with their sad blue eyes. She knew that they were mourning because they had no souls, and she thought within herself that even in prison it was better to belong to the Æsir than to be a mermaid or an Ellewoman, were they ever so free or happy.

While she was still occupied with these thoughts she heard her name spoken, and a bird with large wings flew in at the window, and, smoothing its feathers, stood upright before her. It was Loki in Freyja's garment of feathers, and he made her understand in a moment that he had come to set her free, and that there was no time to lose. He told her to conceal her casket carefully in her bosom, and then he said a few words over her, and she found herself changed into a sparrow, with the casket fastened among the feathers of her breast.

Then Loki spread his wings once more, and flew out of the window, and Idūna followed him. The sea-wind blew cold and rough, and her little wings fluttered with fear; but she struck them bravely out into the air and flew like an arrow over the water.

"This way lies Asgard," cried Loki, and the word gave her strength. But they had not gone far when a sound was heard above the sea, and the wind, and the call of the sea-birds. Thiassi had put on his eagle plumage, and was flying after them. For five days and five nights the three flew over the water that divides Jötunheim from Asgard, and, at the end of every day, they were closer together, for the giant was gaining on the other two.

All the five days the dwellers in Asgard stood on the walls of the city watching. On the sixth evening they saw a falcon and a sparrow, closely pursued by an eagle, flying towards Asgard.

"There will not be time," said Bragi, who had been calculating the speed at which they flew. "The eagle will reach them before they can get into the city."

But Odin desired a fire to be lighted upon the walls; and Thor and Tyr, with what strength remained to them, tore up the trees from the groves and gardens, and made a rampart of fire all round the city. The light of the fire showed Idūna her husband and her friends waiting for her. She made one last effort, and, rising high up in the air above the flames and smoke, she passed the walls, and dropped down safely at the foot of Odin's throne. The giant tried to follow; but, wearied with his long flight, he was unable to raise his enormous bulk sufficiently high in the air. The flames scorched his wings as he flew through them, and he fell among the flaming piles of wood, and was burnt to death.

How Idūna feasted the Æsir on her apples, how they grew young and beautiful again, and how spring, and green leaves, and music came back to the grove, I must leave you to imagine, for I have made my story long enough already; and if I say any more you will fancy that it is Bragi who has come among you, and that he has entered on his endless story.

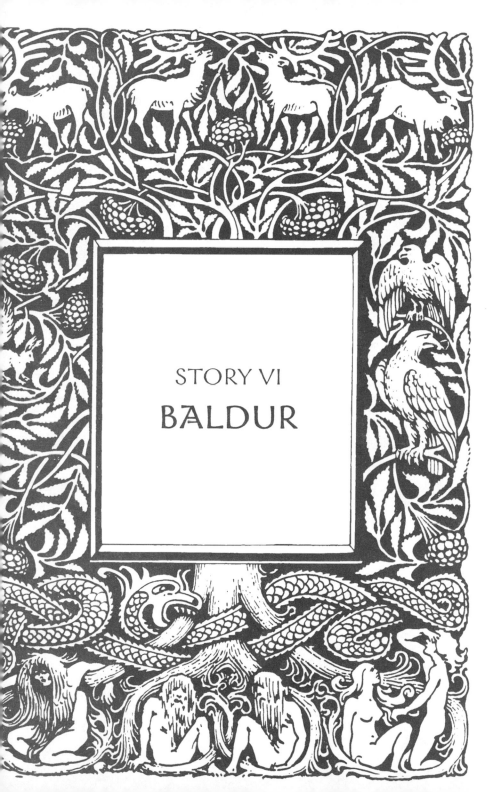

STORY VI
BALDUR

PART I

The Dream

pon a summer's afternoon it happened that Baldur the Bright and Bold, beloved of men and Æsir, found himself alone in his palace of Broadblink. Thor was walking low down among the valleys, his brow heavy with summer heat; Frey and Gerda sported on still waters in their cloud-leaf ship; Odin, for once, slept on the top of Air Throne; a noon-day stillness pervaded the whole earth; and Baldur in Broadblink, the wide-glancing most sunlit of palaces, dreamed a dream.

Now the dream of Baldur was troubled. He knew not whence nor why; but when he awoke he found that a most new and weighty care was within him. It was so heavy that Baldur could scarcely carry it, and yet he pressed it closely to his heart, and said, "Lie there, and do not fall on any one but me." Then he rose up, and walked out from the expanded splendour of his hall, that he might seek his own mother, Frigga, and tell her what had happened to him. He found her in her crystal saloon, calm and kind, waiting to listen, and ready to sympathise; so he walked up to her, his hands pressed closely on his heart, and lay down at her feet sighing.

"What is the matter, dear Baldur?" asked Frigga, gently.

"I do not know, mother," answered he. "I do not know what the matter is; but I have a shadow in my heart."

"Take it out, then, my son, and let me look at it," replied Frigga.

"But I fear, mother, that if I do it will cover the whole earth."

Then Frigga laid her hand upon the heart of her son that she might feel the shadow's shape. Her brow became clouded as she felt it; her parted lips grew pale, and she cried out, "Oh! Baldur, my beloved son! the shadow is the shadow of death!"

Then said Baldur, "I will die bravely, my mother."

But Frigga answered, "You shall not die at all; for I will not sleep to-night until everything on earth has sworn to me that it will neither kill nor harm you."

So Frigga stood up, and called to her everything on earth that had power to hurt or slay. First she called all metals to her; and heavy iron-ore came lumbering up the hill into the crystal hall, brass and gold, copper, silver, lead, and steel, and stood before the Queen, who lifted her right hand high in the air, saying, "Swear to me that you will not injure Baldur;" and they all swore, and went. Then she called to her all stones; and huge granite came with crumbling sand-stone, and white lime, and the round, smooth stones of the sea-shore, and Frigga raised her arm, saying, "Swear that you will not injure Baldur;" and they swore, and went. Then Frigga called to her the trees; and wide-spreading oak-trees, with tall ash and sombre firs came rushing up the hill, with long branches, from which green leaves like flags were waving, and Frigga raised her hand, and said, "Swear that you will not hurt Baldur;" and they said, "We swear," and went. After this Frigga called to her the diseases, who came blown thitherward by poisonous winds on wings of pain, and to the sound of moaning. Frigga said to them, "Swear:" and they sighed, "We swear," then flew away. Then Frigga called to her all beasts, birds, and venomous snakes, who came to her and swore, and disappeared. After this she stretched out her hand to Baldur, whilst a smile spread over her face, saying, "And now, my son, you cannot die."

But just then Odin came in, and when he had heard from Frigga the whole story, he looked even more mournful than

Then Frigga called to her all beasts,
birds, and venomous snakes, —

she had done; neither did the cloud pass from his face when he was told of the oaths that had been taken.

"Why do you still look so grave, my lord?" demanded Frigga, at last. "Baldur cannot now die."

But Odin asked very gravely, "Is the shadow gone out of our son's heart, or is it still there?"

"It cannot be there," said Frigga, turning away her head resolutely, and folding her hands before her.

But Odin looked at Baldur, and saw how it was. The hands pressed to the heavy heart, the beautiful brow grown dim. Then immediately he arose, saddled Sleipnir, his eight-footed steed, mounted him, and, turning to Frigga, said, "I know of a dead Vala (a prophetess), Frigga, who, when she was alive, could tell what was going to happen; her grave lies on the east side of Helheim, and I am going there to awake her, and ask whether any terrible grief is really coming upon us."

So saying Odin shook the bridle in his hand, and the Eight-footed, with a bound, leapt forth, rushed like a whirlwind down the mountain of Asgard, and then dashed into a narrow defile between rocks.

Sleipnir went on through the defile a long way, until he came to a place where the earth opened her mouth. There Odin rode in and down a broad, steep, slanting road which led him to the cavern Gnipa, and the mouth of the cavern Gnipa yawned upon Niflheim. Then thought Odin to himself, "My journey is already done." But just as Sleipnir was about to leap through the jaws of the pit, Garm, the voracious dog who was chained to the rock, sprang forward, and tried to fasten himself upon Odin. Three times Odin shook him off, and still Garm, as fierce as ever, went on with the fight. At last Sleipnir leapt, and Odin thrust just at the same moment; then horse and rider cleared the entrance, and turned eastward toward the dead Vala's grave, dripping blood along the road as they went; while the beaten Garm stood baying in the cavern's mouth.

When Odin came to the grave he got off his horse, and stood with his face northwards looking through barred enclosures into the city of Helheim itself. The servants of Hela were very busy there making preparations for some new guest—hanging gilded couches with curtains of anguish

The voracious dog......sprang forward,
and tried to fasten himself upon Odin

and splendid misery upon the walls. Then Odin's heart died within him and he began to repeat mournful runes in a low tone to himself.

The dead Vala turned heavily in her grave at the sound of his voice, and, as he went on, sat bolt upright. "What man is this," she asked, "who dares disturb my sleep?"

Then Odin, for the first time in his life, said what was not true; the shadow of Baldur dead fell upon his lips, and he made answer, "My name is Vegtam, the son of Valtam."

"And what do you want from me?" asked the Vala.

"I want to know," replied Odin, "for whom Hela is making ready that gilded couch in Helheim?"

"That is for Baldur the Beloved," answered the dead Vala. "Now go away, and let me sleep again, for my eyes are heavy."

But Odin said, "Only one word more. Is Baldur going to Helheim?"

"Yes, I've told you that he is," answered the Vala.

"Will he never come back to Asgard again?"

"If everything on earth should weep for him," answered she, "he will go back; if not, he will remain in Helheim."

Then Odin covered his face with his hands, and looked into darkness.

"Do go away," said the Vala, "I'm so sleepy; I cannot keep my eyes open any longer."

But Odin raised his head, and said again, "Only tell me this one thing. Just now, as I looked into darkness, it seemed to me as if I saw one on earth who would not weep for Baldur. Who was it?"

At this the Vala grew very angry and said, "How couldst *thou* see in darkness? I know of only one who, by giving away his eye, gained light. No Vegtam art thou, but Odin, chief of men."

At her angry words Odin became angry too, and called out as loudly as ever he could, "No Vala art thou, nor wise woman, but rather the mother of three giants."

"Go, go!" answered the Vala, falling back in her grave; "no man shall waken me again until Loki have burst his chains and Ragnarök be come." After this Odin mounted the Eight-footed once more, and rode thoughtfully towards home.

Tales of Norse Mythology

PÃRT II

The Peacestead

hen Odin came back to Asgard, Hermod took the bridle from his father's hand, and told him that the rest of the Æsir were gone to the Peacestead—a broad, green plain which lay just outside the city. Now this was, in fact, the playground of the Æsir, where they practised trials of skill one with another, and held tournaments and sham fights. These last were always conducted in the gentlest and most honourable manner; for the strongest law of the Peacestead was, that no angry blow should be struck, or spiteful word spoken, upon the sacred field; and for this reason some have thought it might be well if children also had a Peacestead to play in.

Odin was too much tired by his journey from Helheim to go to the Peacestead that afternoon; so he turned away, and shut himself up in his palace of Gladsheim. But when he was gone, Loki came into the city by another way, and hearing from Hermod where the Æsir were, set off to join them.

When he got to the Peacestead, Loki found that the Æsir were standing round in a circle shooting at something, and he peeped between the shoulders of two of them to find out what it was. To his surprise he saw Baldur standing in the midst, erect and calm, whilst his friends and brothers were aiming their weapons at him. Some hewed at him with their swords—others threw stones at him—some shot arrows pointed with steel, and Thor continually swung Miölnir at his head. "Well," said Loki to himself, "if this is the sport of Asgard, what must that of Jötunheim be? I wonder what Father Odin and Mother Frigga would say if they were here?" But as Loki still looked, he became even more surprised, for the sport went on, and Baldur was not hurt. Arrows aimed at his very heart glanced back again untinged with blood. The stones fell down from his broad bright brow, and left no bruises there. Swords clave, but did not wound him; Miölnir struck him, and he was not crushed. At this Loki grew perfectly furious with envy and hatred. "And why is Baldur to be so honoured," said he, "that even steel and stone shall not hurt him?" Then Loki changed himself into a little, dark, bent, old woman, with a stick in his hand, and hobbled away from the Peacestead to Frigga's cool saloon. At the door he knocked with his stick.

"Come in!" said the kind voice of Frigga, and Loki lifted the latch.

Now when Frigga saw, from the other end of the hall, a little, bent, crippled, old woman, come hobbling up her crystal floor, she got up with true queenliness, and met her half way, holding out her hand, and saying in the kindest manner, "Pray sit down, my poor old friend; for it seems to me that you have come from a great way off."

"That I have, indeed," answered Loki in a tremulous, squeaking voice.

"And did you happen to see anything of the Æsir," asked Frigga, "as you came?"

"Just now I passed by the Peacestead, and saw them at play."

"What were they doing?"

"Shooting at Baldur."

Then Frigga bent over her work with a pleased smile on her face. "And nothing hurt him?" she said.

"Nothing," answered Loki, looking keenly at her.

"No, nothing," murmured Frigga, still looking down and speaking half musingly to herself; "for all things have sworn to me that they will not."

"Sworn!" exclaimed Loki, eagerly; "what is that you say? Has everything sworn then?"

"Everything," answered she, "excepting, indeed, the little shrub mistletoe, which grows, you know, on the west side of Valhalla, and to which I said nothing, because I thought it was too young to swear."

"Excellent!" thought Loki; and then he got up.

"You're not going yet, are you?" said Frigga, stretching out her hand and looking up at last into the eyes of the old woman.

"I'm quite rested now, thank you," answered Loki in his squeaky voice, and then he hobbled out at the door, which clapped after him, and sent a cold gust into the room. Frigga shuddered, and thought that a serpent was gliding down the back of her neck.

When Loki had left the presence of Frigga, he changed himself back to his proper shape, and went straight to the west side of Valhalla, where the mistletoe grew. Then he opened his knife, and cut off a large branch, saying these words,

> *"Too young for Frigga's oaths,*
> *But not too weak for Loki's work."*

After which he set off for the Peacestead once more, the mistletoe in his hand. When he got there he found that the Æsir were still at their sport, standing round, taking aim, and talking eagerly, and Baldur did not seem tired.

But there was one who stood alone, leaning against a tree, and who took no part in what was going on. This was Hödur, Baldur's blind twin-brother; he stood with his head bent downwards, silent, whilst the others were speaking, doing nothing when they were most eager; and Loki thought that there was a discontented expression on his face, just as if he were saying to himself, "Nobody takes any notice of me." So Loki went up to him, and put his hand upon his shoulder.

"And why are you standing here all alone, my brave friend?" said he. "Why don't you throw something at Baldur? Hew at him with a sword, or show him some attention of that sort."

"I haven't got a sword," answered Hödur, with an impatient gesture; "and you know as well as I do, Loki, that Father Odin does not approve of my wearing warlike weapons, or joining in sham fights, because I am blind."

"Oh! is that it?" said Loki. "Well, I only know I shouldn't like to be left out of everything. However, I've got a twig of mistletoe here which I'll lend you if you like; a harmless little twig enough, but I shall be happy to guide your arm if you would like to throw it, and Baldur might take it as a compliment from his twin-brother."

"Let me feel it," said Hödur, stretching out his uncertain hands.

"This way, this way, my dear friend," said Loki, giving him the twig. "Now, as hard as ever you can, to do *him honour*; throw!"

Hödur threw—Baldur fell, and the shadow of death covered the whole earth.

PART III
Baldur Dead

ne after another they turned and left the Peacestead, those friends and brothers of the slain. One after another they turned and went towards the city; crushed hearts, heavy footsteps, no word amongst them, a shadow upon all. The shadow was in Asgard too,—had walked through Frigga's hall, and seated itself upon the threshold of Gladsheim. Odin had just come out to look at it, and Frigga stood by in mute despair as the Æsir came up.

"Loki did it! Loki did it!" they said at last in confused, hoarse whispers, and they looked from one to another, upon Odin, upon Frigga, upon the shadow which they saw before them, and which they felt within. "Loki did it! Loki, Loki!" they went on saying; but it was no use repeating the name of Loki over and over again when there was another name they were too sad to utter which yet filled all their hearts—Baldur. Frigga said it first, and then they all went to look at him lying down so peacefully on the grass—dead, dead.

"Carry him to the funeral pyre!" said Odin, at length; and four of the Æsir stooped down, and lifted their dead brother.

With scarcely any sound they carried the body tenderly to the sea-shore, and laid it upon the deck of that majestic ship called Ringhorn, which had been *his*. Then they stood round waiting to see who would come to the funeral. Odin came, and on his shoulders sat his two ravens, whose croaking drew clouds down over the Asa's face, for Thought and Memory sang one sad song that day. Frigga came,—Frey, Gerda, Freyja, Thor, Hœnir, Bragi, and Idūna. Heimdall came sweeping over the tops of the mountains on Golden Mane, his swift, bright steed. Ægir the Old groaned from under the deep, and sent his daughters up to mourn around the dead. Frost Giants and Mountain Giants came crowding round the rimy shores of Jötunheim to look across the sea upon the funeral of an Asa. Nanna came, Baldur's fair young wife; but when she saw the dead body of her husband her own heart broke with grief, and the Æsir laid her beside him on the stately ship. After this Odin stepped forward, and placed a ring on the breast of his son, whispering something at the same time in his ear; but when he and the rest of the Æsir tried to push Ringhorn into the sea before setting fire to it, they found that their hearts were so heavy they could lift nothing. So they beckoned to the giantess Hyrrokin to come over from Jötunheim and help them. She, with a single push, set the ship floating, and then, whilst Thor stood up holding Miölnir high in the air, Odin lighted the funeral pile of Baldur and of Nanna.

So Ringhorn went out floating towards the deep, and the funeral fire burnt on. Its broad red flame burst forth towards heaven; but when the smoke would have gone upward too, the winds came sobbing and carried it away.

PART IV
Helheim

hen at last the ship Ringhorn had floated out so far to sea that it looked like a dull, red lamp on the horizon, Frigga turned round and said, "Does any one of you, my children, wish to perform a noble action, and win my love for ever?"

"I do," cried Hermod, before any one else had time to open his lips.

"Go, then, Hermod," answered Frigga, "saddle Sleipnir with all speed, and ride down to Helheim; there seek out Hela, the stern mistress of the dead, and entreat her to send our beloved back to us once more."

Hermod was gone in the twinkling of an eye, not in at the mouth of the earth and through the steep cavern down which Odin went to the dead Vala's grave; he chose another way, though not a better one; for, go to Helheim how you will, the best is but a downward road, and so Hermod found it—downward, slanting, slippery, dark and very cold. At last he came to the Giallar Bru—that sounding river which flows between the living and the dead, and the bridge over which is paved with stones of glittering gold. Hermod was surprised to see gold in such a place; but as he rode over the bridge, and looked down carefully at the stones, he saw that they were only tears which had been shed round the beds of the dying—only tears, and yet they made the way seem brighter. But when Hermod reached the other end of the bridge, he found the courageous woman who, for ages and ages, had been sitting there to watch the dead go by, and she stopped him saying, "What a noise you make. Who are you? Yesterday five troops of dead men went over the Giallar Bridge, and did not shake it so much as you have done. Besides," she added, looking more closely at Hermod, "you are not a dead man at all. Your lips are neither cold nor blue. Why, then, do you ride on the way to Helheim?"

"I seek Baldur," answered Hermod. "Tell me, have you seen him pass?"

"Baldur," she said, "has ridden over the bridge; but there below, towards the north, lies the way to the Abodes of Death."

So Hermod went on the way until he came to the barred gates of Helheim itself. There he alighted, tightened his saddle-girths, remounted, clapped both spurs to his horse, and cleared the gate by one tremendous leap. Then Hermod found himself in a place where no living man had ever been before—the City of the Dead. Perhaps you think there is a great silence there, but you are mistaken. Hermod thought he had never in his life heard so much noise; for the echoes of all words were speaking together—words, some newly uttered and some ages old; but the dead men did not hear who flitted up and down the dark streets, for their ears had been stunned and become cold long since. Hermod rode on through the city until he came to the palace of Hela, which stood in the midst. Precipice was its threshold, the entrance-hall, Wide Storm, and yet Hermod was not too much afraid to seek the innermost rooms; so he went on to the banqueting-hall, where Hela sat at the head of her table, and served her newest guests. Baldur, alas! sat at her right-hand, and on her left his pale young wife. When Hela saw Hermod coming up the hall she smiled grimly, but beckoned to him at the same time to sit down, and told him that he might sup that night with her. It was a strange supper for a living man to sit down

Tales of Norse Mythology

to. Hunger was the table; Starvation, Hela's knife; Delay, her man; Slowness, her maid; and Burning Thirst, her wine. After supper Hela led the way to the sleeping apartments. "You see," she said, turning to Hermod, "I am very anxious about the comfort of my guests. Here are beds of unrest provided for all, hung with curtains of weariness, and look how all the walls are furnished with despair."

So saying she strode away, leaving Hermod and Baldur together. The whole night they sat on those unquiet couches and talked. Hermod could speak of nothing but the past, and as he looked anxiously round the room his eyes became dim with tears. But Baldur seemed to see a light far off, and he spoke of what was to come.

The next morning Hermod went to Hela, and entreated her to let Baldur return to Asgard. He even offered to take his place in Helheim if she pleased; but Hela only laughed at this, and said, "You talk a great deal about Baldur, and boast how much every one loves him; I will prove now if what you have told me be true. Let everything on earth, living or dead, weep for Baldur and he shall go home again; but if *one* thing only refuse to weep, then let Helheim hold its own; he shall *not* go."

"Every one will weep willingly," said Hermod, as he mounted Sleipnir, and rode towards the entrance of the city. Baldur went with him as far as the gate, and began to send messages to all his friends in Asgard, but Hermod would not listen to many of them.

"You will so soon come back to us," he said, "there is no use in sending messages."

So Hermod darted homewards, and Baldur watched him through the bars of Helheim's gateway as he flew along.

"Not soon, not soon," said the dead Asa; but still he saw the light far off, and thought of what was to come.

PART V
Weeping

ell, Hermod, what did she say?" asked the Æsir from the top of the hill, as they saw him coming; "make haste and tell us what she said." And Hermod came up.

"Oh! is that all?" they cried, as soon as he had delivered his message. "Nothing can be more easy;" and then they all hurried off to tell Frigga. She was weeping already, and in five minutes there was not a tearless eye in Asgard.

"But this is not enough," said Odin; "the whole earth must know of our grief that it may weep with us."

Then the father of the Æsir called to him his messenger maidens—the beautiful Valkyrior—and sent them out into all worlds with these three words on their lips, "Baldur is dead!" But the words were so dreadful that at first the messenger maidens could only whisper them in low tones as they went along, "Baldur is dead!" The dull, sad sounds flowed back on Asgard like a new river of grief, and it seemed to the Æsir as if they now wept for the first time—"Baldur is dead!"

"What is that the Valkyrior are saying?" asked the men and women in all the country round, and when they heard rightly, men left their labour and lay down to weep—women dropped the buckets they were carrying to the well, and, leaning their faces over them, filled them with tears. The children crowded upon the doorsteps, or sat down at the corners of the streets, crying as if their own mothers were dead.

The Valkyrior passed on. "Baldur is dead!" they said to the empty fields; and straightway the grass and the wild field-flowers shed tears. "Baldur is dead!" said the messenger maidens to the rocks and the stones; and the very stones began to weep. "Baldur is dead!" the Valkyrior cried; and even the old mammoth's bones, which had lain for centuries under the hills, burst into tears, so that small rivers gushed forth from every mountain's side. "Baldur is dead!" said the messenger maidens as they swept over silent sands; and all the shells wept pearls. "Baldur is dead!" they cried to the sea, and to Jötunheim across the sea; and when the giants understood it, even they wept, whilst the sea rained spray to heaven. After this the Valkyrior stepped from one stone to another until they reached a rock that stood alone in the middle of the sea; then, all together, they bent forward over the edge of it, stooped down and peeped over, that they might tell the monsters of the deep. "Baldur is dead!" they said; and, the sea monsters and the fish wept. Then the messenger maidens looked at one another, and said, "Surely our work is done." So they twined their arms round one another's waists, and set forth on the downward road to Helheim, there to claim Baldur from among the dead.

Now after he had sent forth his messenger maidens, Odin had seated himself on the top of Air Throne that he might see how the earth received his message. At first he watched the Valkyrior as they stepped forth north and south, and east and west; but soon the whole earth's steaming tears rose up like a great cloud, and hid everything from him. Then he looked down through the cloud, and said, "Are you all weeping?" Then Valkyrior heard the sound of his voice as they went all together down the slippery road, and they turned round, stretching out their arms towards Air Throne, their long hair falling back, whilst, with choked voices and streaming eyes, they answered, "The world weeps, Father Odin; the world and we."

After this they went on their way until they came to the end of the cave Gnipa, where Garm was chained, and which yawned over Niflheim. "The world weeps," they said one to another by way of encouragement, for here the road was so dreadful; but just as they were about to pass through the mouth of Gnipa they came upon a haggard witch named Thaukt, who sat in the entrance with her back to them, and her face towards the abyss. "Baldur is dead! Weep, weep!" said the messenger maidens, as they tried to pass her; but Thaukt made answer,

> *"What she doth hold,*
> *Let Hela keep;*
> *For naught care I,*
> *Though the world weep,*
> *O'er Baldur's bale.*
> *Live he or die*
> *With tearless eye,*
> *Old Thaukt shall wail."*

And with these words leaped into Niflheim with a yell of triumph.

"Surely that cry was the cry of Loki," said one of the maidens; but another pointed towards the city of Helheim, and there they saw the stern face of Hela looking over the wall.

"One has not wept," said the grim Queen, "and Helheim holds its own." So saying she motioned the maidens away with her long, cold hand.

Then the Valkyrior turned and fled up the steep way to the foot of Odin's throne, like a pale snowdrift that flies before the storm.

After this a strong child, called Vali, was born in the city of Asgard. He was the youngest of Odin's sons—strong and cold as the icy January blast; but full, also, as it is of the hope of the new year. When only a day old he slew the blind Hödur by a single blow, and then spent the rest of his life in trying to lift the shadow of death from the face of the weeping earth.

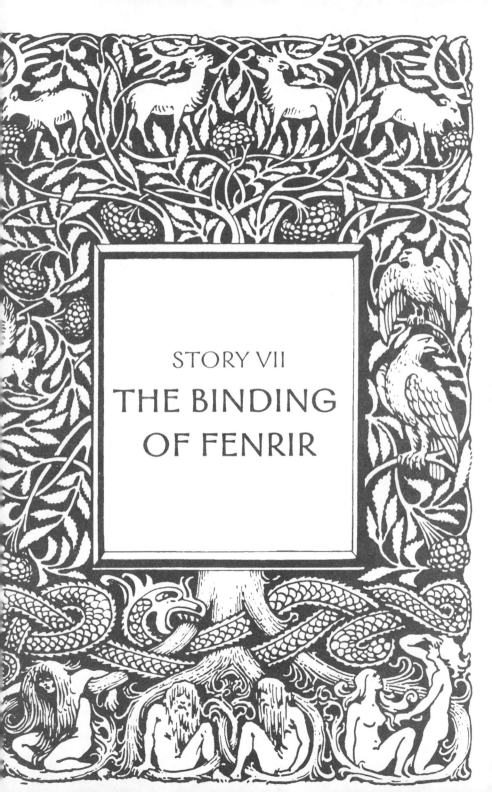

STORY VII

THE BINDING
OF FENRIR

PART I

The Might of Asgard

 hope you have not forgotten what I told you of Fenrir, Loki's fierce wolf-son, whom Odin brought home with him to Asgard, and of whose reformation, uncouth and wolfish as he was, All-Father entertained some hope, thinking that the wholesome, bright air of Gladsheim, the sight of the fair faces of the Asyniur and the hearing of the brave words which day by day fell from the lips of heroes, would, perhaps, have power to change the cruel nature he had inherited from his father, and make him worthy of his place as a dweller in the City of Lords.

To Tyr, the brave and strong-handed, Odin assigned the task of feeding Fenrir, and watching him, lest, in his cruel strength, he should injure any who were unable to defend themselves. And truly it was a grand sight, and one that Asa Odin loved, to see the two together, when, in the evening after the feast was over in Valhalla, Fenrir came prowling to Tyr's feet to receive his food from the one hand strong enough to quell him.

Tyr stood up in his calm strength like a tall, sheltering rock in which the timid sea-birds find a home; and Fenrir roared and howled round him like the bitter, destroying wave that slowly undermines its base.

Time passed on. Tyr had reached the prime of his strength; but Fenrir went on growing, not so rapidly as to awaken fear, as his brother Jörmungand had done, but slowly, surely, continually—a little stronger and a little fiercer every day.

The Æsir and the Asyniur had become accustomed to his presence; the gentlest lady in Asgard no longer turned away from the sight of his fierce mouth and fiery eye; they talked to each other about the smallest things, and every daily event was commented on and wondered about; but no one said anything of Fenrir, or noticed how gradually he grew, or how the glad air and the strong food, which gave valour and strength to an Asa, could only develop with greater rapidity fierceness and cruelty in a wolf. And they would have gone on living securely together while the monster grew and grew, if it had not been that Asa Odin's one eye, enlightened as it was by the upspringing well of wisdom within, saw more clearly than the eyes of his brothers and children.

One evening, as he stood in the court of Valhalla watching Tyr as he gave Fenrir his evening meal, a sudden cloud of care fell on the placid face of All-Father, and when the wolf, having satisfied his hunger, crouched back to his lair, he called together a council of the heads of the Æsir—Thor, Tyr, Bragi, Hœnir, Frey, and Niörd; and, after pointing out to them the evil which they had allowed to grow up among them unnoticed, he asked their counsel as to the best way of overcoming it before it became too strong to withstand.

Thor, always ready, was the first to answer. "One would think," he said, "to hear the grave way in which you speak, Father Odin, that there was no such thing as a smithy near Asgard, or that I, Asa Thor, had no power to forge mighty weapons, and had never made my name known in Jötunheim as the conqueror and binder of monsters. Set your mind at rest. Before to-morrow evening at this time I will have forged a chain with which you shall bind Fenrir; and, once bound in a chain of my workmanship, there will be nothing further to fear from him."

The assembled Æsir applauded Thor's speech; but the cloud did not pass away from Odin's brow.

"You have done many mighty deeds, Son Thor," he said; "but, if I mistake not, this binding of Fenrir will prove a task too difficult even for you."

Thor made no answer; but he seized Miölnir, and, with sounding steps, strode to the smithy. All night long the mighty blows of Miölnir rang on the anvil, and the roaring bellows breathed a hot blast over all the hill of Asgard. None of the Æsir slept that night; but every now and then one or other of them came to cheer Thor at his work. Sometimes Frey brought his bright face into the dusky smithy; sometimes Tyr entreated permission to strike a stout blow; sometimes Bragi seated himself among the workers, and, with his eyes fixed on the glowing iron, poured forth a hero song, to which the ringing blows kept time.

There was also another guest, who, at intervals, made his presence known. By the light of the fire the evil form of Fenrir was seen prowling round in the darkness, and every now and then a fiendish, mocking laugh filled the pauses of the song, and the wind, and the ringing hammer.

All that night and the next day Thor laboured and Fenrir watched, and, at the time of the evening meal, Thor strode triumphantly into Father Odin's presence, and laid before him Læding, the strongest chain that had ever yet been forged on earth. The Æsir passed it from one to another, and wondered at its immense length, and at the ponderous moulding of its twisted links.

"It is impossible for Fenrir to break through this," they said; and they were loud in their thanks to Thor and praises of his prowess; only Father Odin kept a grave, sad silence.

When Fenrir came into the court to receive his food from Tyr, it was agreed that Thor and Tyr were to seize and bind him. They held their weapons in readiness, for they expected a fierce struggle; but, to their surprise, Fenrir quietly allowed the chain to be wound round him, and lay down at his ease, while Thor, with two strokes of Miölnir, riveted the last link into one of the strongest stones on which the court rested. Then, when the Æsir were about to congratulate each other on their victory, he slowly raised his ponderous form, which seemed to dilate in the rising, with one bound forward snapped the chain like a silken thread, and walked leisurely to his lair, as if no unusual thing had befallen him.

The Æsir, with downcast faces, stood looking at each other. Once more Thor was the first to speak. "He who breaks through Læding," he said, "only brings upon himself the still harder bondage of Dromi." And having uttered these words, he again lifted Miölnir from the ground, and, weary as he was, returned to the smithy and resumed his place at the anvil.

For three days and nights Thor worked, and, when he once more appeared before Father Odin, he carried in his hand Dromi—the "Strong Binding." This chain exceeded Læding in strength by one-half, and was so heavy that Asa Thor himself staggered under its weight; and yet Fenrir showed no fear of allowing himself to be bound by it, and it cost him very little more effort than on the first evening to free himself from its fetters.

After this second failure Odin again called a council of Æsir in Gladsheim, and Thor stood among the others, silent and shamefaced.

It was now Frey who ventured first to offer an opinion. "Thor, Tyr, and other brave sons of the Æsir," he said, "have passed their lives valiantly in fighting against giants and monsters, and, doubtless, much wise lore has come to them through these adventures. I, for the most part, have spent my time peacefully in woods and fields, watching how the seasons follow each other, and how the silent, dewy night ever leads up the brightly-smiling day; and, in this watching, many things have been made plain to me which have not, perhaps, been thought worthy of regard by my brother Lords. One thing that I have learned is, the wondrous strength that lies in little things, and that the labour carried on in darkness and silence ever brings forth the grandest birth. Thor and Miölnir have failed to forge a chain strong enough to bind Fenrir; but, since we cannot be helped by the mighty and renowned, let us turn to the unknown and weak.

"In the caverns and dim places of the earth live a tiny race of people, who are always working with unwearied, noiseless fingers. With Asa Odin's permission, I will send my messenger, Skirnir, and entreat aid of them; and we shall, perhaps, find that what passes the might of Asgard may be accomplished in the secret places of Svartheim."

The face of Asa Odin brightened as Frey spoke, and, rising immediately from his seat, he broke up the council, and entreated Frey to lose no time in returning to Alfheim and despatching Skirnir on his mission.

PART II

The Secret of Svartheim

I n spite of the cloud that hung over Asgard all was fair and peaceful in Alfheim. Gerda, the radiant Alf Queen, made there perpetual sunshine with her bright face. The little elves loved her, and fluttered round her, keeping up a continual merry chatter, which sounded through the land like the sharp ripple of a brook over stony places; and Gerda answered them in low, sweet tones, as the answering wind sounds among the trees.

These must have been pleasant sounds to hear after the ringing of Miölnir and the howling of Fenrir; but Frey hardly gave himself time to greet Gerda, and his elves, before he summoned Skirnir into his presence, and acquainted him with the danger that hung over Asgard, and the important mission which the Æsir had determined to trust to his sagacity. Skirnir listened, playing with the knot of his wondrous sword, as he was wont to do, in order to make known to every one that he possessed it; for, to confess the truth, it was somewhat too heavy for him to wield.

"This is a far different mission," he said, "from that on which you once sent me—to woo fairest Gerda; but, as the welfare of Asgard requires it, I will depart at once, though I have little liking for the dark caves and cunning people."

Frey thanked him, and, putting a small key into his hand, which was, indeed, the key to the gate of Svartheim, he bade him farewell, and Skirnir set out on his journey.

The road from Alfheim to Svartheim is not as long as you would be apt to imagine. Indeed, it is possible for a careless person to wander from one region to another without being at once aware of it. Skirnir, having the key in his hand, took the direct way. The entrance-gate stands at the opening of a dim mountain-cave. Skirnir left his horse without, and entered; the air was heavy, moist, and warm, and it required the keenest glances of Skirnir's keen eyes to see his way. Innumerable narrow, winding paths, all leading downwards, opened themselves before him. As he followed the widest, a faint clinking sound of hammers met his ear, and, looking round, he saw groups of little men at work on every side. Some were wheeling small wheelbarrows full of lumps of shining metal along the ledges of the rock: some, with elfin pick-axes and spades, were digging ore from the mountain-side; some, herded together in little caves, were busy kindling fires, or working with tiny hammers on small anvils. As he continued his downward path the last remnant of daylight faded away; but he was not in total darkness, for now he perceived that each worker carried on his head a lantern, in which burned a pale, dancing light. Skirnir knew that each light was a Will-o'-the-wisp, which the dwarf who carried it had caught and imprisoned to light him in his work during the day, and which he must restore to the earth at night.

For many miles Skirnir wandered on lower and lower. On every side of him lay countless heaps of treasure—gold, silver, diamonds, rubies, emeralds—which the cunning workers stowed away silently in their dark hiding-places. At length he came to the very middle of the mountain, where the rocky roof rose to an immense height, and where he found himself in a brilliantly-lighted palace. Here, in truth, were hung all the lights in the world, which, on dark, moonless nights, are carried out by dwarfs to deceive the eyes of men. Corpse-lights, Will-o'-the-wisps, the sparks from glow-worms' tails, the light in fire-flies' wings—these, carefully hung up in tiers round and round the hall, illuminated the palace with a cold blue light, and revealed to Skirnir's eyes the grotesque and hideous shapes of the tiny beings around him. Hump-backed, cunning-eyed, open-mouthed, they stood round, laughing, and whispering, and pointing with shrivelled fingers. One among them, a little taller than the rest, who sat on a golden seat thickly set with diamonds, appeared to be a kind of chief among them, and to him Skirnir addressed his message.

Cunning and wicked as these dwarfs were, they entertained a wholesome fear of Odin, having never forgotten their one interview with him in Gladsheim; and, therefore, when they heard from whom Skirnir came, with many uncouth gesticulations they bowed low before him, and declared themselves willing to obey All-Father's commands. They asked for two days and two nights in which to complete their task, and during that time Skirnir remained their guest in Svartheim.

He wandered about, and saw strange sights. He saw the great earth central fire, and the swarthy, withered race, whose task it is ceaselessly to feed it with fuel; he saw the diamond-makers, who change the ashes of the great fire into brilliants; and the dwarfs, whose business it is to fill the cracks in the mountain-sides with pure veins of silver and gold, and lead them up to places where they will one day meet the eyes of men. Nearer the surface he visited the workers in iron and the makers of salt-mines; he drank of their strange-tasting mineral waters, and admired the splendour of their silver-roofed temples and dwellings of solid gold.

At the end of two days Skirnir re-entered the audience-hall, and then the chief of the dwarfs put into his hand a slender chain. You can imagine what size it was when I tell you that the dwarf chief held it lightly balanced on his forefinger; and when it rested on Skirnir's hand it felt to him no heavier than a piece of thistle-down.

The Svart King laughed loud when he saw the disappointment on Skirnir's face. "It seems to you a little thing," he said; "and yet I assure you that in making it we have used up all the materials in the whole world fit for the purpose. No such chain can ever be made again, neither will the least atom of the substances of which it is made be found more. It is fashioned out of six things. The noise made by the footfall of cats; the beards of women; the roots of stones; the sinews of bears; the breath of fish; and the spittle of birds. Fear not with this to bind Fenrir; for no stronger chain will ever be made till the end of the world."

Skirnir now looked with wonder at his chain, and, after having thanked the dwarfs, and promised to bring them a reward from Odin, he set forth on his road home, and, by the time of the evening meal, reached Valhalla, and gladdened the hearts of the Æsir by the tidings of his success.

PART III

Honour

ar away to the north of Asgard, surrounded by frowning mountains, the dark lake, Amsvartnir, lies, and, above the level of its troubled waters, burns Lyngvi, the island of sweet broom, flaming like a jewel on the dark brow of Hela. In this lonely isle, to which no ship but Skidbladnir could sail, the Æsir, with Fenrir in the midst, assembled to try the strength of the dwarfs' chain.

Fenrir prowled round his old master, Tyr, with a look of savage triumph in his cruel eyes, now licking the hand that had so long fed him, and now shaking his great head, and howling defiantly. The Æsir stood at the foot of Giöll, the sounding rock, and passed Gleipnir, the chain, from one to another, talking about it, while Fenrir listened. "It was much stronger than it looked," they said; and Thor and Tyr vied with each other in their efforts to break it; while Bragi declared his belief that there was no one among Æsir or giants capable of performing so great a feat, "unless," he added, "it should be you, Fenrir."

This speech roused the pride of Fenrir; and, after looking long at the slender chain and the faces of the Æsir, he answered, "Loath am I to be bound by this chain; but, lest you should doubt my courage, I will consent that you should bind me, provided one of you put his hand into my mouth as a pledge that no deceit is intended."

There was a moment's silence among the Æsir when they heard this, and they looked at one another. Odin looked at Thor, and Thor looked at Bragi, and Frey fell behind, and put his hand to his side, where the all-conquering sword, which he alone could wield, no longer rested.

At length Tyr stepped forward valiantly, and put his strong right hand, with which he had so often fed him, into the wolf's cruel jaws.

At this signal the other Æsir threw the chain round the monster's neck, bound him securely with one end, and fastened the other to the great rock Giöll. When he was bound Fenrir rose, and shook himself, as he had done before; but in vain he raised himself up, and bounded forward—the more he struggled the more firmly the slender chain bound him.

At this sight the Æsir set up a loud shout of joy; for they saw their enemy conquered, and the danger that threatened Asgard averted. Only Tyr was silent, for in the struggle he had lost his hand.

Then Thor thrust his sword into the mouth of Fenrir, and a foaming dark flood burst forth, roared down the rock and under the lake, and began its course through the country a turbid river. So it will roll on till Ragnarök be come.

The sails of Skidbladnir now spread themselves out to the wind; and the Æsir, seated in the magic ship, floated over the lake silently in the silent moonlight; while, from the top of Bifröst, over the Urda fount and the dwelling of the Norns, a song floated down. "Who," asked one voice, "of all the Æsir has won the highest honour?" and, singing, another voice made answer, "Tyr has won the highest honour; for, of all the Æsir, he has the most worthily employed his gift."

"Frey gave his sword for fairest Gerda."

"Odin bought for himself wisdom at the price of his right eye."

"Tyr, not for himself, but for others, has sacrificed his strong right hand."

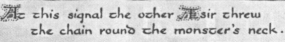
At this signal the other Æsir threw
the chain round the monster's neck.

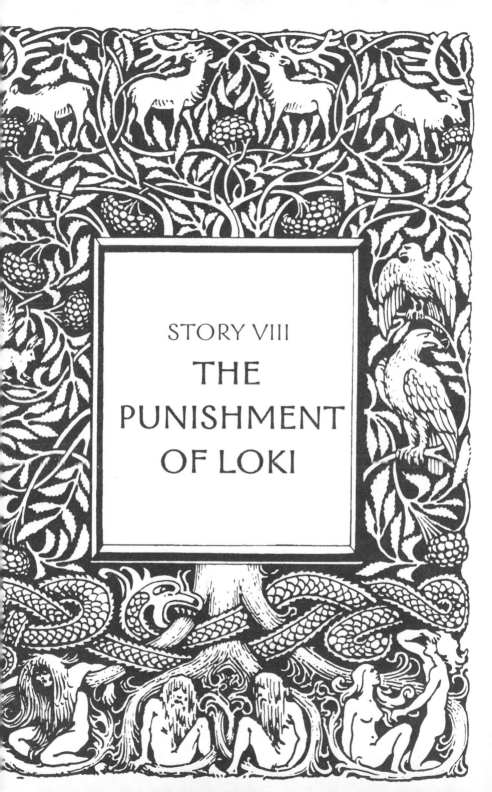

STORY VIII

THE
PUNISHMENT
OF LOKI

The Punishment of Loki

fter the death of Baldur, Loki never again ventured to intrude himself into the presence of the Æsir. He knew well enough that he had now done what could never be forgiven him, and that, for the future, he must bend all his cunning and vigilance to the task of hiding himself for ever from the eyes of those whom he had so injured, and escaping the just punishment he had brought upon himself.

"The world is large, and I am very cunning," said Loki to himself, as he turned his back upon Asgard, and wandered out into Manheim; "there is no end to the thick woods, and no measure for the deep waters; neither is there any possibility of counting the various forms under which I shall disguise myself. All-Father will never be able to find me; I have no cause to fear." But, though Loki repeated this over and over again to himself, he was afraid.

He wandered far into the thick woods, and covered himself with the deep waters; he climbed to the tops of misty hills, and crouched in the dark of hollow caves; but above the wood, and through the water, and down into the darkness, a single ray of calm, clear light seemed always to follow him, and he knew that it came from the eye of All-Father, who was watching him from Air Throne.

Then he tried to escape the judging eye by disguising himself under various shapes. Sometimes he was an eagle on a lonely mountain-crag; sometimes he hid himself as one among a troop of timid reindeer; sometimes he lay in the nest of a wood-pigeon; sometimes he swam, a bright-spotted fish, in the sea; but, wherever he was, among living creatures, or alone with dead nature, everything seemed to know him, and to find some voice in which to say to him, "You are Loki, and you have killed Baldur." Air, earth, or water, there was no rest for him anywhere.

Tired at last of seeking what he could nowhere find, Loki built himself a house by the side of a narrow, glittering river which, at a lower point, flashed down from a high rock into the sea below. He took care that his house should have four doors in it, that he might look out on every side, and catch the first glimpse of the Æsir when they came, as he knew they would come, to take him away. Here his wife, Siguna, and his two sons, Ali and Nari, came to live with him.

Siguna was a kind woman, far too good and kind for Loki. She felt sorry for him now that she saw he was in great fear, and that every living thing had turned against him, and she would have hidden him from the just anger of the Æsir if she could; but the two sons cared little about their father's dread and danger; they spent all their time in quarrelling with each other; and their loud, angry voices, sounding above the waterfall, would speedily have betrayed the hiding-place, even if All-Father's piercing eye had not already discovered it. If only the children would be quiet, Siguna used to say anxiously every day; but Loki said nothing; he was beginning to know by experience that there was that about his children that could never be kept quiet or hidden away.

At last, one day when he was sitting in the middle of his house looking alternately out of all the four doors, and amusing himself as well as he could by making a fishing net, he spied in the distance the whole company of the Æsir approaching his house. The sight of them coming all together—beautiful, and noble, and free—pierced Loki with a pang that was worse than death. He rose without daring to look again, threw his net on a fire that burned on the floor, and, rushing to the side of the little river, he turned himself into a salmon, swam down to the deepest, stillest pool at the bottom, and hid himself between two stones. The Æsir entered the house, and looked all round in vain for Loki, till Kvasir, one of Odin's sons, famous for his keen sight, spied out the remains of the fishing-net in the fire; then Odin knew at once that there was a river near, and that it was there where Loki had hidden himself. He ordered his sons to make a fresh net, and to cast it into the water, and drag out whatever living thing they could find there. It was done as he desired. Thor held one end of the net, and all the rest of the Æsir drew the other through the water. When they pulled it up the first time, however, it was empty, and they would have gone away disappointed, had not Kvasir, looking earnestly at the meshes of the net, discovered that something living had certainly touched them. They then added a weight to the net, and threw it with such force that it reached the bottom of the river, and dragged up the stones in the pool.

Loki now saw the danger he was in of being caught in the net, and, as there was no other way of escape, he rose to the surface, swam down the river as quickly as he could, and leaped over the net into the waterfall. He swam and leaped quickly as a flash of lightning, but not so quickly but that the Æsir saw him, knew him through his disguise, and resolved that he should no longer escape them. They divided into two bands. Thor waded down the river to the waterfall; the other Æsir stood in a group below. Loki swam backwards and forwards between them. Now he thought he would dart out into the sea, and now that he would spring over the net back again into the river. This last seemed the readiest way of escape, and, with the greatest speed, he attempted it. Thor, however, was watching for him, and, as soon as Loki leaped out of the water, he stretched out his hand, and caught him while he was yet turning in the air. Loki wriggled his slippery, slimy length through Thor's fingers; but the Thunderer grasped him tightly by the tail, and, holding him in this manner in his hand, waded to the shore. There Father Odin and the other Æsir met him; and, at Odin's first searching look, Loki was obliged to drop his disguise, and, cowering and frightened, to stand in his proper shape before the assembled Lords. One by one they turned their faces from him; for, in looking at him, they seemed to see over again the death of Baldur the Beloved.

I told you that there were high rocks looking over the sea not far from Loki's house. One of these, higher than the rest, had midway four projecting stones, and to these the Æsir resolved to bind Loki in such a manner that he should never again be able to torment the inhabitants of Manheim or Asgard by his evil-doings. Thor proposed to return to Asgard, to bring a chain with which to bind the prisoner; but Odin assured him that he had no need to take such a journey, "Loki," he said, "has already forged for himself a chain stronger than any you can make. While we have been occupied in catching him, his two sons, Ali and Nari, transformed into wolves by their evil passions, have fought with, and destroyed, each other. With their sinews we must make a chain to bind their father, and from that he can never escape."

It was done as Asa Odin said. A rope was made of the dead wolves' sinews, and, as soon as it touched Loki's body, it turned into bands of iron, and bound him immovably to the rock. Secured in this manner the Æsir left him.

But his punishment did not end here. A snake, whose fangs dropped venom, glided to the top of the rock, and leaned his head over to peer at Loki.

The eyes of the two met and fixed each other. The serpent could never move away afterwards; but every moment a burning drop from his tongue fell down on Loki's shuddering face.

In all the world there was only one who pitied him. His kind wife ever afterwards stood beside him, and held a cup over his head to catch the poison. When the cup was full, she was obliged to turn away to empty it, and drops of poison fell again on Loki's face He shuddered and shrank from it, and the whole earth trembled. So will he lie bound till Ragnarök be come.

In all the world there was only one
who pitied him.

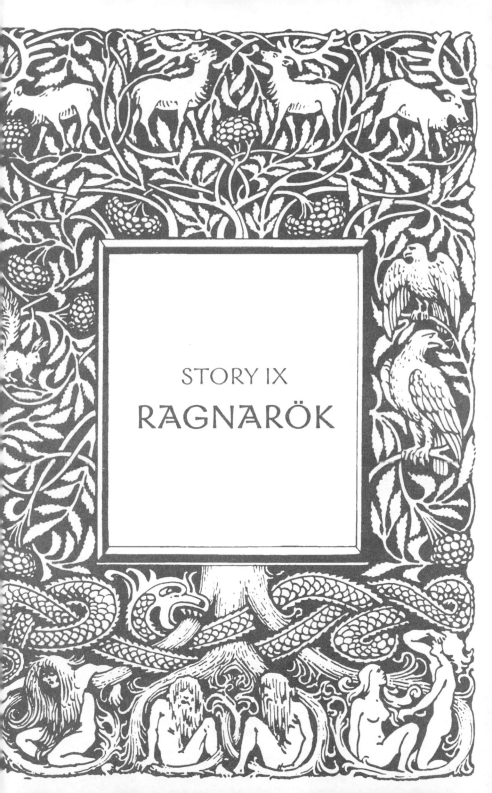

STORY IX
RAGNARÖK

The Twilight of the Gods

ince the day that Baldur died no one had walked in the bright halls of Broadblink—no one had even stepped through the expanded gates. Instead of undimmed brightness, a soft, luminous mist now hung over the palace of the dead Asa, and the Asyniur whispered to one another that it was haunted by wild dreams.

"I have seen them," Freyja used to say; "I have seen them float in at sunset through the palace windows and the open doors; every evening I can trace their slight forms through the rosy mist; and I know that those dreams are wild and strange from the shuddering that I feel when I look at them, or if ever they glance at me."

So the Asyniur never went into Broadblink, and though the Æsir did not think much about the dreams, they never went there either.

But one day it happened that Odin stood in the opening of the palace gates at sunset. The evening was clear and calm, and he stood watching the western sky until its crimson faded into soft blue grey; then the colours of the flowers began to mix one with another—only the tall white and yellow blossoms stood out alone—the distance became more dim. It was twilight, and there was silence over the earth whilst the night and the evening drew near to one another. Then a young dream came floating through the gates into Broadblink. Her sisters were already there; but she had only just been born, and, as she passed Odin, she touched him with a light hand, and drew him along with her into the palace. She led him into the same hall in which Baldur had dreamed, and there Odin saw the night sky above him, and the broad branches of Yggdrasil swaying in the breeze. The Norns stood under the great ash; the golden threads had dropped from their fingers; and Urd and Verdandi stood one on each side of Skuld, who was still veiled. For a long time the three stood motionless, but at length Urd and Verdandi raised each a cold hand, and lifted the veil slowly from Skuld's face. Odin looked breathlessly within the veil, and the eyes of Skuld dilated as he looked, grew larger and larger, melted into one another, and, at last, expanded into boundless space.

In the midst of space lay the world, with its long shores, and vast oceans, ice mountains, and green plains; Æsirland in the midst, with Manheim all round it; then the wide sea, and, far off, the frost-bound shores of Jötunheim. Sometimes there was night and sometimes day; summer and winter gave place to one another; and Odin watched the seasons as they changed, rejoiced in the sunshine, and looked calmly over the night.

But at last, during one sunrise, a wolf came out of Jarnvid, and began to howl at the sun. The sun did not seem to heed him, but walked majestically up the sky to her mid-day point; then the wolf began to run after her, and chased her down the sky again to the low west. There the sun opened her bright eye wide, and turned round at bay; but the wolf came close up to her, and opened his mouth, and swallowed her up. The earth shuddered, and the moon rose. Another wolf was waiting for the moon with wide jaws open, and, while yet pale and young, he, too, was devoured. The earth shuddered again; it was covered with cold and darkness, while frost and snow came driving from the four corners of heaven. Winter and night, winter and night, there was now nothing but winter.

A dauntless eagle sat upon the height of the Giantess' Rock, and began to strike his harp. Then a light red cock crowed over the Bird Wood. A gold-combed cock crowed over Asgard and over Helheim a cock of sooty red. From a long way underground Garm began to howl, and at last Fenrir broke loose from his rock-prison, and ran forth over the whole earth. Then brother contended with brother, and war had no bounds. A hard age was that.

> "An axe age,
> A sword age,
> Shields oft cleft in twain;
> A storm age,
> A wolf age,
> Ere the earth met its doom."

Confusion rioted in the darkness. At length Heimdall ran up Bifröst, and blew his Giallar horn, whose sound went out into all worlds, and Yggdrasil, the mighty ash, was shaken from its root to its summit. After this Odin saw himself ride forth from Asgard to consult Mimer at the Well of Wisdom. Whilst he was there Jörmungand turned mightily in his place, and began to plough the ocean, which caused it to swell over every shore, so that the world was covered with water to the base of its high hills. Then the ship Naglfar was seen coming over the sea with its prow from the east, and the giant Hrym was the steersman.

All Jötunheim resounded, and the dwarfs stood moaning before their stony doors. Then heaven was cleft in twain, and a flood of light streamed down upon the dark earth. The sons of Muspell, the sons of fire, rode through the breach, and at the head of them rode the swarth Surt, their leader, before and behind whom fire raged, and whose sword outshone the sun. He led his flaming bands from heaven to earth over Bifröst, and the tremulous bridge broke in pieces beneath their tread. Then the earth shuddered again; even giantesses stumbled; and men trod the way to Helheim in such crowds that Garm was sated with their blood, broke loose, and came up to earth to look upon the living. Confusion rioted, and Odin saw himself, at the head of all the Æsir, ride over the tops of the mountains to Vigrid, the high, wide battle-field, where the giants were already assembled, headed by Fenrir, Garm, Jörmungand, and Loki. Surtur was there, too, commanding the sons of fire, whom he had drawn up in several shining bands on a distant part of the plain.

Then the great battle began in earnest. First, Odin went forth against Fenrir, who came on, opening his enormous mouth; the lower jaw reached to the earth, the upper one to heaven, and would have reached further had there been space to admit of it. Odin and Fenrir fought for a little while only, and then Fenrir swallowed the Æsir's Father; but Vidar stepped forward, and, putting his foot on Fenrir's lower jaw, with his hand he seized the other, and rent the wolf in twain. In the meantime Tyr and Garm had been fighting until they had killed each other. Heimdall slew Loki, and Loki slew Heimdall. Frey, Beli's radiant slayer, met Surtur in battle, and was killed by him. Many terrible blows were exchanged ere Frey fell; but the Fire King's sword outshone the sun, and where was the sword of Frey? Thor went forth against Jörmungand; the strong Thunderer raised his arm—he feared no evil—he flung Miölnir at the monster serpent's head. Jörmungand leaped up a great height in the air, and fell down to the earth again without life; but a stream of venom poured forth from his nostrils as he died. Thor fell back nine paces from the strength of his own blow; he bowed his head to the earth, and was choked in the poisonous flood; so the monster serpent was killed by the strong Thunderer's hand; but in death Jörmungand slew his slayer.

Then all mankind forsook the earth, and the earth itself sank down slowly into the ocean. Water swelled over the mountains, rivers gurgled through thick trees, deep currents swept down the valleys—nothing was to be seen on the earth but a wide flood. The stars fell from the sky, and flew about hither and thither. At last, smoky clouds drifted upward from the infinite deep, encircling the earth and the water; fire burst forth from the midst of them, red flames wrapped the

 Thor went forth against Jörmungand.

world, roared through the branches of Yggdrasil, and played against heaven itself. The flood swelled, the fire raged; there was now nothing but flood and fire.

"Then," said Odin, in his dream, "I see the end of all things. The end is like the beginning, and it will now be for ever as if nothing had ever been."

But, as he spoke, the fire ceased suddenly; the clouds rolled away; a new and brighter sun looked out of heaven; and he saw arise a second time the earth from ocean. It rose slowly as it had sunk. First, the waters fell back from the tops of new hills that rose up fresh and verdant; raindrops like pearls dripped from the freshly budding trees, and fell into the sea with a sweet sound; waterfalls splashed glittering from the high rocks; eagles flew over the mountain streams; earth arose spring-like; unsown fields bore fruit; there was no evil, and all nature smiled. Then from Memory's Forest came forth a new race of men, who spread over the whole earth, and who fed on the dew of the dawn. There was also a new city on Asgard's Hill—a city of gems; and Odin saw a new hall standing in it, fairer than the sun, and roofed with gold. Above all, the wide blue expanded, and into that fair city came Modi and Magni, Thor's two sons, holding Miölnir between them. Vali and Vidar came, and the deathless Hœnir; Baldur came up from the deep, leading his blind brother Hödur peacefully by the hand; there was no longer any strife between them. Two brothers' sons inhabited the spacious Wind-Home.

Then Odin watched how the Æsir sat on the green plain, and talked of many things. "Garm is dead," said Hödur to Baldur, "and so are Loki, and Jörmungand, and Fenrir, and the world rejoices; but did our dead brothers rejoice who fell in slaying them?"

"They did, Hödur," answered Baldur; "they gave their lives willingly for the life of the world;" and, as he listened, Odin felt that this was true; for, when he looked upon that beautiful and happy age, it gave him no pain to think that he must die before it came—that, though for many, it was not for him.

By and bye Hœnir came up to Hödur and Baldur with something glittering in his hand—something that he had found in the grass; and as he approached he said, "Behold the golden tablets, my brothers, which in the beginning of time were given to the Æsir's Father, and were lost in the Old World."

Then they all looked eagerly at the tablets, and, as they bent over them, their faces became even brighter than before.

"There is no longer any evil thing," said Odin; "not an evil sight, nor an evil sound."

But as he spoke dusky wings rose out of Niflheim, and the dark-spotted serpent, Nidhögg, came flying from the abyss, bearing dead carcases on his wings—cold death, undying.

Then the joy of Odin was drowned in the tears that brimmed his heart, and it was as if the eternal gnawer had entered into his soul. "Is there, then, no victory over sin?" he cried. "Is there no death to Death?" and with the cry he woke. His dream had faded from him. He stood in the palace gates alone with night, and the night was dying. Long since the rosy clasp of evening had dropped from her; she had turned through darkness eastward, and looked earnestly towards dawn. It was twilight again, for the night and the morning drew near to one another. A star stood in the east—the morning star—and a coming brightness smote the heavens. Out of the light a still voice came advancing, swelling, widening, until it filled all space. "Look forth," it said, "upon the groaning earth, with all its cold, and pain, and cruelty, and death. Heroes and giants fight and kill each other; now giants fall, and heroes triumph; now heroes fall, and giants rise; they can but combat, and the earth is full of pain. Look forth, and fear not; but when the worn-out faiths of nations shall totter like old men, turn eastward, and behold the light that lighteth every man; for there is nothing dark it doth not lighten; there is nothing hard it cannot melt; there is nothing lost it will not save."